DO YOU SOMETIMES FEEL LIKE A NOBODY?

Campus Life Books

DO YOU SOMETIMES FEEL LIKE A
N⊘BODY?
TIM STAFFORD

A DIVISION OF CTI
CampusLife *BOOKS* / TYNDALE HOUSE PUBLISHERS, INC. WHEATON, ILLINOIS

Second Tyndale House printing, March 1987
Library of Congress Catalog Card Number 85-52123
ISBN 0-8423-0594-7
Copyright © 1980 by Campus Life Books, a division of CTi

CONTENTS

FOREWORD

Before you begin reading, I want you to know something basic: I can't solve problems for you. Every solution must begin with your decision to make it work.

So you must not look at this book as a potential savior. It can point you in the right direction, but only you can take the first step.

I wish you would think of this as a kind of emotional coloring book. If you pick up a coloring book just to admire it, you'll be bored. As art, it isn't much. It just provides guidelines so learners can begin to discover themselves as artists. This book gives the outline; you give it color, in your own way.

In preparing this book, I have drawn on many different articles from *Campus Life* Magazine, as well as other books and magazines. Different personalities and points of view come through, and some of the chapters are by different authors. But the basic point of view is my own; where no byline is given, I am the direct author. I hope that it will prod you and encourage you to become closer to the remarkable person God made you to be.

—Tim Stafford

Acknowledgments

Grateful acknowledgment is given to the publishers for use of the following material:

"I Wish I'd Reached Her." From *Is There a Place I Can Scream?* by Harold Myra. Copyright © 1975 by Harold Myra. Used by permission of Tyndale House Publishers.

"Advice for Eleanor" by John Piper. From *The Reformed Journal*. Copyright © 1978 by Wm. B. Eerdmans Publishing Company. Used by permission.

"I Am a Beautiful Girl." From *Love Yourself: Self-Acceptance and Depression* by Walter Trobisch. Copyright © 1976 by InterVarsity Press. Used by permission.

Scripture quotations from *The Living Bible*. Copyright © 1971 by Tyndale House Publishers.

Chapter 1:

HATING YOURSELF

I Am a Beautiful Girl

■ The girl entered our hotel room. It was the day after my wife and I had given a lecture at a university in northern Europe. The hotel room was the only place we had for counseling.

She was a beautiful Scandinavian girl. Long blond hair fell over her shoulders. Gracefully she sat down in the armchair offered to her and looked at us with deep and vivid blue eyes.

Rick Smolan

Her long arms allowed her to fold her hands over her knees. We noticed her fine, slender fingers, revealing a very tender, precious personality.

As we discussed her problems, we came back again and again to one basic issue which seemed to be the root of all the others. It was the problem which we had least expected when she entered the room: She could not love herself. In fact, she hated herself to such a degree that she was only one step away from putting an end to her life.

To point out to her the apparent gifts she had—her success as a student, the favorable impression she had made upon us by her outward appearance—seemed to be of no avail. She refused to acknowledge anything good about herself. She was afraid that any self-appreciation she might express would mean giving in to the temptation of pride, and to be proud meant to be rejected by God. She had grown up in a tight-laced religious family and had learned that self-depreciation was Christian and self-rejection the only way to find acceptance by God.

We asked her to stand up and take a look in the mirror. She turned her head away. With gentle force I held her head so that she had to look into her own eyes. She cringed as if she were experiencing physical pain.

It took a long time before she was able to whisper, though unconvinced, the sentence I asked her to repeat, "I am a beautiful girl."

∎

—Walter Trobisch
Love Yourself

The Sounds of Ugliness

David Strickler

■The sound of ugliness is mostly silent.
You can hear it when people's conversation stops
   as a crippled person crosses their path.
You can hear it in the hopelessness on a girl's face
   as she looks in the mirror.
You can hear it when a girl sits next to a guy with a
   bad complexion and automatically turns to the person on
      the other side, not wanting, really, to talk to a guy who
         looks like that, so awkward and uncomfortable about
            himself.
You can hear it in the hesitation before a guy slides into the
   back seat of a car, jammed in next to the girl who's
      overweight.
The fat people can hear the silent song of ugliness all day.
The people with deformed bodies can hear it.
The people with plain faces and skeletons the wrong size or
   bodies the wrong shape can hear it.
Even the beautiful, who cannot believe in their own beauty,
   can hear it.
If the sound of ugliness could be heard all the time, by
   everyone, it would make such a chorus of groanings, of
      self-hating sighs, of sadness, that I think we could hear
         little of anything else.

Do you hear this ugly sound?
Do you recognize it dribbling from your own mouth?
Even today, when you're afraid to talk to someone new,
   afraid to get your picture taken, do you hear the sound?
Some people hate all of themselves; most hate only a part.
Do you hate your smile?
Your shyness? Your race? Your brain?
What is it that bothers you?
Have you faced the way you feel about it?
Have you honestly asked,
   "How can anyone—especially God—love me the way I am?"

Those who never face themselves
   are like people trying to use a map
      without knowing where they are.   ■

Ugly
Clear to the Bone

■ "Beauty may only be skin deep, but ugliness goes clear to the bone." There's truth as well as humor in that. Ugliness doesn't just happen on the surface. Sooner or later it gets to *you*, to the person underneath that skin.

Ugliness can make you think your soul looks ugly—that's how it goes to the bone.

Take my friend John. My first memory of him goes back to

a childhood family picnic. The day was hot, and I got stuffed into the back seat next to him. He was fat and sweaty and took up more than his share of the space. I disliked him immediately: disliked being stuffed stickily next to him, and I resented his shape.

Later we became friends and spent many hours fishing together in the California mountains. I learned to look beyond his extra weight and see the real person inside. After a while I never noticed his shape. Yet we never discussed his problem. I suppose each of us was too wrapped up in his own fears to think about someone else's.

So I didn't know how John felt until years later. We were in the Colorado Rockies then, climbing up ravines and over boulders. Breathing hard, we reached the summit of the steep ridge we were on and stopped to enjoy the panorama beneath us. It was then John asked me, with heavy emotion behind the question, "Do you still think of me as fat?"

The question startled me. You see, he'd lost his excess weight years before and had turned into a trim, good-looking person. "No, not at all," I said. And for the first time we opened up to each other about our feelings. He told me he still thought of himself as fat and ugly. He was so used to seeing ugliness in the mirror that he had to look hard to see the new person. Fat still affected the way he thought about himself and the way he acted with girls. He expected people to be repulsed by him.

His ugliness had gone to the bone. He'd cured the surface problem, but underneath, ugliness survived.

This is the way self-hate gets started for many of us. The standards of good looks, popularity, and success are so high, who can measure up? Who can keep some of the ugliness from going clear to the bone?

And once there, the ugliness is hard to get out. In extreme cases, it cripples you and makes you useless. In milder cases, it cuts the heart out of living. ∎

DO YOU SOMETIMES FEEL LIKE A NOBODY?

The Self-Hate Cycle

It has been described as an endless cycle,
 with no way out:
Because we think we are worthless,
 we are wrapped up in ourselves
  and cannot love others.
Because we cannot really love others,
 but only love them from "duty,"
  they don't love us back.
Because others don't love us,
 or we project that their love, like ours,
  is fake,
   we think we are worthless.
How are we going to escape
 this self-pitying cycle?

David Kreider

The Starling in the Drainpipe

■ Ugliness is more than the way you look.

I can still remember, vividly, dumb things I did in the third grade.

Can you?

I cried when we lost a football game. Only babies cried. I was so ashamed of myself, I can still cringe thinking of it.

I got called "four-eyes." That most senseless of all insults hurt me. I still remember.

My brother announced bitterly that I was my father's favorite. He was so sure, and I felt so shocked and guilty. It wasn't true, but I still remember.

Why are we so ready to remember the things that hurt?

Why so ready to believe that we are ugly when the truth is that God made us beautiful?

Why do our minds carry us back to the pain, forgetting what friends we had, what games we won, what fun we enjoyed?

It seems we are waiting from birth to be hurt into self-hate.

Are you really worthless?

For everything you do wrong, how many things do you do right?

When you do something right—
  help a friend, pass a test, get to school on time—

Gregg Lewis

it should, by a simple reflex,
  make you feel good!
Give yourself a pat on the back!
But for many people, like the beautiful Scandinavian girl
  Walter Trobisch told of,
    the girl who could not call herself beautiful,
      the reflex is badly damaged.
We give ourselves no credit for what we do right,
  pick out flaws
    magnify mistakes
      make ourselves miserable.
Who can love something so prone to be unhappy?
Can even God?

And what about sin?
Or what about the part of me that's dumb
  or truly ugly,
    mean, unhappy,
      a failure at everything,
        the part that doesn't care
          about God,
            the part that's a bad friend.
Can anybody love *that*?

Once, when I was a little boy,
  a baby starling fell from its nest
    in our drainpipe.
We found him
  by following the squalling chirps.
He lay by the side of the house,
  and he wasn't a pretty sight.
He had a mouth that opened bigger than his body,
  and thick, dark pinfeathers scattered
    over a bare, pink skin.
His wings, with immature feathers,
  rubbed in the dirt but couldn't move him.
He couldn't stand.
All he did was tell us, noisily,
  how bad things were.

We took him inside
  and kept him on the back porch
    in a coffee can.
We dipped white bread in milk
  and put the soggy pieces in his wide mouth.
He ate ravenously, constantly.
One morning we heard no hoarse cries,
  and his tiny body was still.
We buried him in a solemn funeral,
  under the maple tree that grew
    in the middle of our back yard.

I loved that starling.
It didn't matter
  that he was ugly and weak.
I only wanted him to eat
  and grow strong and learn to fly.
It wouldn't have made any sense to say
  that I loved all of him
    except for the ugly parts.
The ugly parts were part of him,
  and I loved all of him.
Lord, I come

DO YOU SOMETIMES FEEL LIKE A NOBODY?

new-born, ugly, hungry,
   with wings that can't fly.
Will you feed me, love me,
  help me mend?
You healed lepers, blind men;
  I can't heal starlings, let alone myself.
But you can,
  you who love me—
    ugly me.
Help me mend.   ■

Chapter 2:
THINKING RIGHT

Wallowitch

Humble Rob

■ When he was small, a brother had stuck an arrow in his eye. He hadn't lost his sight, but one eye stayed in its own direction. His family life wasn't good, either, so he had some serious problems. But he became, by some measures, a model Christian. He took seriously the words Paul wrote in Galatians 2:20: "I have been crucified with Christ and I no longer live, but Christ lives in me." He followed that for all he was worth.

As he understood it, his old, problem-riddled self was dead and gone. Christ was now his life, living in him like a hand in a glove. All he had to do was believe it was so, forcing his mind completely away from those old problems. They weren't there any more. He should think of them as imagined bogeymen under a bed; he should ignore them and think of something else—of Christ.

Sometimes—you might even say often—the fears and self-pity would come back to him. You could see it on his face. But from what he understood of the Bible, he couldn't permit them. If you asked him how he was doing, he would say—in faith—that he was doing fine, praising the Lord. After all, if his life was Christ's, wasn't it truly fine?

Unfortunately, he would sink lower and lower until finally he had to admit that he was going through a genuine crisis. He would call for help, usually to the little group of Christians who gathered on Thursdays, tearfully telling them how he had failed to yield to Christ, had not trusted in Christ's death, had let the "old man" come to life. The group would turn their attention to him, putting their hands on him and praying for him. They would pray for him throughout the week, telephoning him to see how he was. And usually, under the flood of all that attention, he would get back on track again. Until the next crisis, that is, which usually seemed to be worse than the last one.

Rob really didn't seem to be making any progress. In fact, he slipped backward—he seemed to need more and more attention each time. And you couldn't help wondering what he was really asking for. Was it the prayer or the attention?

Yet I am convinced that Rob was absolutely sincere and tried with all his might to put his own deep problems aside. The trouble was, he couldn't do it. ■

What Becomes of
Ugly
Feelings?

■ Does it really matter how we feel about ourselves?
Yes, it does.
If you think you are junk, you will tend to act like junk.

Some people cannot make friends because they are convinced
they have nothing to offer. They become so terribly focused on their problems they can't escape themselves
to think of others.

Some marry, not really for love, but to try to fill the awful
vacuum inside.

They imagine their self-hating feelings can be iced over
    by gooey, pink frosting of wild romantic feelings.
But if they cannot give to the person they marry,
    the frosting soon melts.

Some stay in jobs that make them unhappy because they are
    afraid to risk failures.
They stay in their jobs and make others around them unhappy.

Some go into work that will help other people, hoping that
    they can feel worthwhile if they sacrifice themselves
        to other people's good.
But they only help others from tired old duty, and their lack
    of real love shows.
Or their work becomes a crusade to build themselves
    up as great humanitarians.

Some try to fill empty spaces in their lives with cars, with
    impressive grades and awards, with clothes, with new,
        wilder experiences.

So long as you think you are nothing,
    so long as you are preoccupied with the impression you
        make, you will find it very hard to love your neighbor
            or to truly love God.

When you sit in your bedroom
    moping,
        feeling sorry for yourself,
            you are as close to being worthless
                as any child of God can ever be.

But you are not nobody
    nothing
        nowhere.
Because God has made you someone
    something
        somewhere
            very precious.   ■

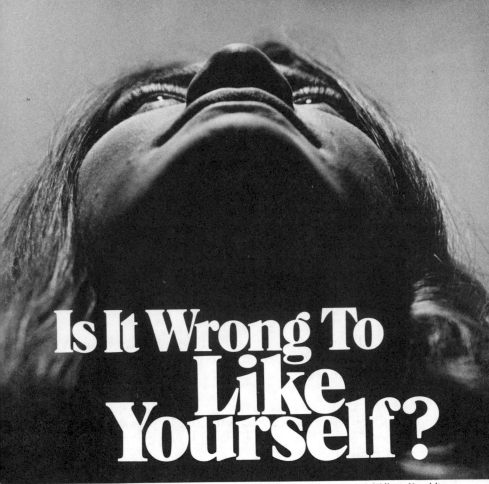

Is It Wrong To Like Yourself?

William Koechling

■ Jesus said these words: "If anyone comes to me and does not hate his father and mother, his wife and children, his brothers and sisters—yes, even *his own life*—he cannot be my disciple" (Luke 14:26). He repeatedly told his followers that they would be unable to find life until they denied themselves, even died to themselves.

So immediately a question arises: If Jesus taught such denial, how can it be right to like yourself? Isn't it the "self" that is the problem in life? Don't we need to get rid of our "self" so that Christ can shine through without interference?

If you "like yourself," aren't you liking the problem?

That line of thinking made Rob intent on ignoring his own feelings about himself. "I used to be led by my feelings, before I was a Christian," he would say, "but now I'm to follow God and live by faith." He believed God had stripped away all his problems on the cross. To go back to those problems by, say, going to a counselor who would talk them through with him, encouraging him to face his own feelings realistically, would in effect "undo" what Christ had done in giving him a new life. The best way was to put his feelings out of the picture entirely, living as though the problems were completely gone.

This trend is part of a whole school of Christian thinking. There are many variations of it, and I am reluctant to disagree with it because there is more than a little truth in it. But some of its popular versions do, I believe, oversimplify the Bible and sometimes hurt people with emotional problems. Without wanting to badmouth them, I will refer to people who believe this as the "Nothings" because they say, repeatedly, "I am nothing; Christ is everything."

Their beliefs are complicated, but I want to point out two important aspects. First, they emphasize that all pride is bad. I think that all Christians would agree that there is a kind of pride that is deadly—the pride that says to God "I am self-sufficient. I don't need you. I'll make it on my own." But Nothings believe in extinguishing all pride—pride in a good job, pride in an act of kindness, pride in an attractive, healthy body. They think it detracts from loving God. They quote Paul: "If I am going to boast, let me boast in the Lord."

Second, Nothings believe that all our problems were destroyed when Jesus died on the cross, and that we are meant to have the full results of that immediately. Thus all problems are religious problems: a person is depressed or discouraged or sick only because he hasn't "yielded" to God, or "put God on the throne of his life," or some other phrase meant to indicate a full realization of Christ's total power in all areas of life.

There is much I could say about Nothings, both good and bad. Although I think they try to make part of the truth the whole truth, they still hold on to part of the truth, and that is worth a lot. In particular, they give all glory to God—and he deserves it.

A Nothing philosophy can work, especially for people blessed with a strong ego and a stable personality. Since these people already tend to think highly of themselves, the Nothing philosophy keeps their feet on the ground. But for Rob, who tends to think *poorly* of himself, it didn't seem to help at all. In fact, while in theory Rob was giving more glory to God by "living by faith," in practice he was giving God a bad reputation. Rob was full of religious talk but almost empty of long-term religious results. It was plain to nearly everyone that he had *not* left his problems behind, and that he needed to deal with them.

Where did Rob go wrong? I think he misunderstood the Bible when it says "If anyone is in Christ, he is a new creation; the old has gone, the new has come!" (2 Cor. 5:17). I do not think, as Nothings do, that when we are converted God does a rabbit-in-the-hat trick and substitutes a different person inside the same body. When we become Christians we stay exactly who we are. We have the same personality, the same abilities, the same likes and dislikes. I never heard of someone who could not shoot free throws before becoming a Christian but could afterward. The changes are more subtle. For example, a new Christian may lose *interest* in shooting free throws if his priorities are no longer wrapped around basketball.

What God makes new is startlingly new: a new state of forgiveness, a new direction in life, a new way of seeing things, a new relationship to God that begins changing things so that, at the end of your life, you're totally different from what you would have been without God. It isn't as though your broken-down '68 Buick is magically transformed into a spanking new one. No, the old car simply begins to get loving care and is set on a new road going a new direction. Besides that, it begins to operate on the right kind of fuel.

The Bible tells Christians to "walk in the Spirit." A walk is not a leap. It is a slow way of getting from one place to another. Rob needed to walk away from his problems. Many of them were deeply rooted in his personality. They were as

DO YOU SOMETIMES FEEL LIKE A NOBODY?

real as the baby in the belly of a pregnant girl or as the stump of an amputee.

The mind has scars as real as the body's. Guilt from sin is instantly destroyed at conversion. Its results are not. Most of those changes take time, though for some people God does seem to instantly wipe them out. Generally he chooses not to.

We are like amnesiacs—people who have been hit on the head by sin so we don't remember our true identity. We wake up in the hospital after God has operated on us, and someone tells us our true name. We are who they say we are. Even our family (whom we don't recognize) tells us it's so. But it may be a long time before we automatically turn when our name is called.

The Bible does tell us that when we accept Jesus' new life, our old selves are dead. But the Bible always clarifies that comment a split second later by telling us to shape up to align our lives with the new reality. Christians have to do this each day, not just the first day of their conversion. They are to patiently reform themselves by the renewing of their minds (Rom. 12:1). They are to keep putting to death what is already dead: their old way of living (Col. 3:3,5). There is a new life for all Christians that is ours for the taking. But learning to understand and use it takes time. Rob needed the time.

Some Christians go even further than Rob. They aren't content with ignoring their "old selves"; they want to "put their old selves to death" by putting themselves down. As Nothings they want to extinguish all pride, so they talk about how sinful and miserable they are, sometimes with satisfied expressions on their faces.

Sometimes this humility seems rather self-centered. June, for instance, would never take a compliment. She was a good singer, but you had to wheedle her into a performance. Then she could only find fault with what she'd done, making apologies and saying, meekly, that she had only done her best. If you said it had sounded good to you, she would only say, "It must have been the Lord."

Her humility, oddly enough, put her on center stage. The attention was on her when you had to persuade her to sing and when she told you how terribly she sang. No one else knew what good singing was; only her opinion was right. By talking glumly about how poorly she'd sung, she attracted compliments, which I suspect she liked to hear.

The worst thing about June and all Nothings who put themselves down as worthless, trying to extinguish pride, is that they disagree with the God who made them. He said men and women were very good (Gen. 1:27,31). Even though people have been sinful and have displayed their disagreeable tendencies for several thousand years, God still loves them (John 3:16). You do not love something that has no value. You may love something that is flawed and broken, just as someone might love a beat-up old car because he sees the original beauty through all the rust and broken glass. But you do not love something that is worthless.

Is it wrong to like yourself? If it is wrong for you, it would seem wrong for God as well. But he makes it very clear that he doesn't just like us, he loves us. How can we disagree with his opinion? How can we extinguish pride in something he is proud of?

This still leaves a question, however. If Rob and June are wrong, who's right? Just what did Jesus mean when he told people to "die to themselves"?

I believe what he meant had little or nothing to do with the way his disciples felt (or feel) about themselves. He wasn't talking about whether you love or hate yourself in the emotional sense. I believe he was speaking to the priorities you choose. To "die to yourself" is to have your leader die and to replace him with Christ. Your old leader is you: you did what made you happy. Now you follow what Jesus wants. The old self, the one before Jesus came to live and give direction, has died. When Jesus comes into someone's life it is a little like the election of a new president. The buildings in Washington stay the same. Most of the people working in the buildings stay the same. But the direction has changed from the top. We call it a "new government." The old policies are dead; the old memos, waste paper. The new president's presence makes things totally different.

Or we could use the analogy Jesus used: a branch grafted into a vine. You used to be a severed branch trying to live without any roots, but the process was hopeless. That era is now over. You don't think any more about what you need to survive "independently." Your only need is to stay grafted into the vine.

The molecular structure of the branch is identical before and after grafting. But who can deny that it is totally different? Before, it was trash, fit for burning. Now it bears beautiful fruit.

This view opens the way for true humility, not false, "putting-yourself-down" humility. In Romans 12, Paul first explains that Christians ought not be conformed to the world but renewed and transformed. He goes on, "I say to every man among you not to think more highly of himself than he ought to think, but to think so as to have sound judgment." He concludes that every person has a unique gift to offer the body of Christ. Please notice that Paul doesn't say Christians shouldn't think highly of themselves. He is concerned that they not think more highly than is justified. They are to form a *realistic* picture of themselves, good and bad. Then they can use their God-given gifts for the good of people around them, as well as eliminate the parts of their lives that are harmful.

This is true humility: a realistic assessment of who I am so that I can be used to glorify God. Where do I get such a realistic picture? I can get it only from listening to God, from listening to wise people who know me, and from careful thinking about myself as I interact with God and others. Sometimes dying to self and coming to Christ may mean giving up constant self-punishment or self-pity, and accepting yourself as God has made you.

God values your life. So should you. He also wants you to change. So should you. He knows your faults, and he knows your gifts. So should you.

Is it wrong to like yourself? Is is wrong to like the parts of yourself that God wants to change? (Though it is wrong to accept those faults as a real part of yourself, let God deal with them in his own way instead of trying to do it yourself.) But it is very right to like the things that God has made and pronounced good. It is right to like your body, your abilities, your gifts—and to turn them over to God, thanking him. ■

Taking Compliments

■ My friend Pat
came home from Ecuador
   and gave us
      a musician playing sadly on the pipes,
         a beautifully carved man standing eighteen inches tall.
We call him Newby, for a reason I forget.

We like him.
We're proud that he's ours.

Sometimes people come to see us
   and they admire Newby.
      "What a beautiful carving!"
So what do I say?
It's a compliment, but
   I didn't carve Newby,
      didn't even have the good taste to
         pick him out.
He was a gift,
   a gift from the carver,
      a gift from my friend.
I deserve no credit.
But still I say "Thank you.
Pat gave him to us."

Sometimes I get other compliments
    on how I look, or talk, or write,
        or think.
Compliments are hard to take.
They're embarrassing.
Half the time I don't believe them.
(They liked that?
    It was horrible.)
I know I don't deserve any credit anyway.
Everything good in me is a gift from God.
He made it.
He picked it out for me.
So what should I say?
"Oh, it really wasn't very good."
"Don't thank me."
No, the right thing to say is
    "Thank you."

And remember that
    whatever you have or do or look like
        is a gift you don't deserve
            but which you ought to be thankful for
                and proud that
                    someone cared enough
                        to give it
                            to you. ■

J. Fred Sharp

■ Just once—
    tomorrow morning, maybe—
        when you wake up,
            your mouth tasting like wool
                and the day outside your window
                    gray and unformed,
                        think about this.

Before you start remembering
    work you didn't get done, or
        worrying whether to wear that
            blue-striped thing or
                the yellow one, or
                    wishing you had all the good looks
                        you'll never have; before all that,
                            think:
Aren't there good reasons to be glad I'm
    waking up as me?
Maybe you have
    pimples
        or feel short
            or your nose is too big.
Ignore the little flaws;
    see the big picture—
        knit your hands together
            and squeeze the finger tight,
                watch them glow red and
                    snap back to normal color when you let go.
Stretch your toes to the foot of the bed—
    your body works.
It works like a marvel, a dream—
    faster than thought, it does what
        you want.
No levers, no steering wheel;
    you think and it's there.
A ball sails high in the air;
    in a second your brain solves
        a half-hour's calculus problem.
You think, "I've got it!"
    and your body is already
        on its way to gather it in.
Without calculation
    a huge muscle called your heart
        accelerates
            to bathe every cell
                (trillions of them) with blood

and your lungs scoop the air
for oxygen
and harvest your blood
for carbon dioxide.
It doesn't happen just
catching a ball.
It happens walking down the hall
or springing from bed in the morning
joyful to be
in your own body.

Take a minute now:
count to yourself
all the people you'll talk to today—
teachers, friends, parents,
brothers, sisters.
Have you ever gone twenty-four hours
without talking to someone?
Each person on earth (billions of them)
is as much a marvel as you,
yet each person needs others.
We work together:
I don't have to reinvent arithmetic
to count my socks
or plant wheat seeds
in order to eat bread next September.
Someone else has already done those things.
Is there a radio near your bed?
Turn it on and another amazing creature will
tell you the weather.
He got it from another
wonderful creature
who got it from instruments
made by another
and invented by yet another wonderful creature
who isn't even alive anymore.
How well off would you be
if this cold morning
you had to do everything alone:

DO YOU SOMETIMES FEEL LIKE A NOBODY?

make your own food,
house,
socks,
car?
Where would you be without all those unseen people?
Isn't it incredible
how we share?

One minute more
before you get out of bed.
Think about one more thing.
Giraffes move gracefully;
bees share the invention of honey;
an antelope leaps more quickly away from a gun than you
can think.
But not a single animal
so far as I know
ever lies awake
in the gray morning,
eyes wide open,
amazed,
thinking
how wonderful it is to wake up as me. ■

Why Is the Bible Silent?

■ There is a problem lurking in all discussions of self-hatred. I am sure some of you have thought of it already. If self-hatred is so crucial, why doesn't the Bible say something about it?

Of course the Bible speaks to self-image; we saw some of the specific passages in "Is It Wrong to Like Yourself?" But even those show good self-image as a natural attitude that people should take for granted.

Nowhere in the Bible is self-hatred treated as a major problem. Polls today show that 75 to 80 percent of teenagers say they struggle with self-hatred. Why, then, must we look so hard in the Bible to find something that directly applies? Every book on self-image I've read avoids this question which seems crucial to me. Nowhere in all his letters to churches, which deal with all kinds of practical questions, does Paul tell Christians to stop putting themselves down. In all his teaching, Jesus never listed "hating yourself" as a problem.

Two important passages are sometimes applied to this sub-

Robert McQuilkin

ject, since they talk about loving yourself. One is Jesus' command in Luke 10:27 to love your neighbor as you love yourself. Similarly Paul's great section on marriage, Ephesians 5:21-33, says "Husbands ought to love their own wives as their own bodies." If you dislike your self and your body, loving your neighbor and your wife as much as you love them would not be a challenging command. So, some argue, Christians ought first to love themselves and their bodies.

But if you look closer at these passages, I think you have to conclude that this conclusion is a misunderstanding. The love called for in those places is not the emotional kind—the way you *feel* about your neighbor or yourself. Rather, Jesus and Paul are talking about active love. Jesus goes on in Luke to explain about loving your neighbor as yourself by telling the story of the Good Samaritan. That story says nothing about how the Good Samaritan felt; he showed love in the form of time, food, and medical care. He may well have felt repulsed by the "differentness" of the man he helped.

In Ephesians 5, Paul goes on to explain his remark about love by saying, "No one ever hated his own body, but he feeds and cares for it." If he were talking about emotional feelings, he would be wrong: some people violently hate their own bodies. The point of both stories is that, regardless of how people feel, they do take care of themselves. They feed themselves. They bathe themselves. They take it easy on a sore leg. And that is just the way we ought to act toward our neighbors or our partners in marriage, regardless of how we feel.

So these two passages, while they don't contradict the importance of emotionally loving yourself, are really irrelevant to it.

Could it be that the people in the Bible never had self-hatred kinds of troubles? No, several Old Testament characters suffered from depression or inferiority complexes. Saul was depressed. Moses put himself down when God called him to talk to Pharaoh. Psalm 31 vividly describes David's extreme discouragement, and 1 Kings 19 shows Elijah so discouraged he asks God to kill him. Jeremiah and Solomon frequently show gloomy personalities in the books they wrote.

You find the normal range of emotions in the Bible. Yet you find no direct answer to problems of self-hatred, a problem that can crush a person's ability to live an effective Christian life.

Why is the Bible silent? One explanation is that feeling bad about yourself never used to be as severe and widespread. Psychology has made people more aware of their feelings. The pressure of modern life is harder to bear. The Bible, then, says no more about this problem than it does about computer technology.

An opposite explanation is that "self-image" is a psychological fad. Christians have picked it up and tried to make the Bible fit, but they can't succeed. The Bible says nothing about it because it's not a great problem. The best advice is to ignore how you feel about yourself and go on with obeying God. To psychoanalyze yourself only compounds the problem.

There is some truth to both these ideas, I think. In Africa, where I am living as I write this, self-hatred doesn't show itself very often, at least not as vividly as I've seen it in America. The problem is, to some extent, caused by modern, industrialized, psychoanalyzed civilization.

And I would also agree that the problem can be overemphasized. Sometimes the cure is worse than the disease. In California, where I used to live, there are large groups of people who are so aware of how they feel that they are quite useless to anyone. I think they end up making themselves unhappy through their introspection. The deeper they look inside, the more of a mess they find.

But I think that both these explanations miss something basic about the Bible. The fact is, the Bible tells little about what is wrong with men. Although it makes clear that there is something wrong, listing all kinds of examples, it doesn't systematically analyze these wrongs. It lumps religion and economics together—worshiping an idol is condemned in the same sentence as depriving a poor person of his rights. Homosexuality and failing to "keep the Sabbath" are treated as almost the same. These and many other equally different actions are simply described as sin, which is rooted in a rejection, and a defiance, of God's will.

The Bible also lumps all true solutions in one: coming into a good relationship with God through Jesus. This style doesn't imply that all people have the same problems, and that God heals each person in the same way. But it keeps the focus on the central theme and lets the details be worked out personally and individually. It makes all advice relevant to every person at all times in history.

There is specific truth, God's truth, that does not appear in the Bible. I drive my car every day based on that kind of truth. My electric lights operate under another non-biblical truth.

Even regarding human behavior, with which the Bible is primarily concerned, there can be new insights not found in the Bible. Where such ideas conflict with the Bible, they ought to be quickly ruled out by Christians. But where they do not obviously conflict, we can ask ourselves whether they fit into the total picture the Bible gives, and whether they are true and helpful.

Two men in particular offered non-Christian insights that, though very different from each other, had enormous effect on the way people think about human problems. Though both men were, I think, frequently wrong, and both badly overstated their cases, they have given some insights that have become second nature to us. I am thinking of Sigmund Freud and Karl Marx.

We can scarcely talk about how people think without using ideas that Freud developed. He developed the idea of an unconscious mind. He showed that we sometimes do things for reasons we're not even aware of. He explored for the first time how crucial our childhood relationship to our parents is, particularly as we form an idea of ourselves as men and women. Though he went overboard on the importance of sexuality, he certainly underlined the fundamental importance of sexuality in our lives. All these are ideas we tend to think of as common sense, and they are—now. But they were not common to people before Freud.

Some of Freud's ideas directly contradict the Bible. But most of what he taught is simply not dealt with there. The Bible implies, of course, that our relationships with parents (and Father God) are crucial. It stresses the importance of sex.

But it hardly analyzes sin in terms of the sexual drive. There are Christians who think very little of Freud, and there are Christians who accept much of his thought. Nearly all of us believe more of his theories than we normally realize. We are at liberty to believe much or a little, because the Bible says little about it.

The Bible does, however, provide the answers Freud could not. Freud's analysis of problems may be helpful, but his psychoanalytic therapy has not proven terribly effective. The Bible offers better help—warmth and stability for families; solid guidelines for marriage so that sexuality can be creatively expressed; confession between Christians (which is something like Freud's psychiatric couch, but is based on genuine love and commitment instead of a pseudo-friendship you have to pay for). Most of all, the Bible provides a Savior who can forgive and heal the past. While not giving Freud's analysis, the Bible gives an answer. It is an answer shaped in love.

Take another example: no set of theories could seem more different from Freud's than Karl Marx's. Marx was unconcerned about the problems of the rich people who could afford Freud's care; he was thinking about the problems of the world, which he analyzed as rooted in an economic class struggle, rich versus poor, workers versus owners. His theories have won at least as many believers as Freud's.

In Marx, too, there is at least a kernel of truth. We have all come to see—many thanks to Marx—that history is controlled, not just by the nobility of leaders, but by the profit margin of national treasuries. We're used to saying that one country is friendly with another because it's to their economic advantage. We even admit that our own motives are greatly affected by how much money we stand to make. We can see that the poor are trying to rise and in many cases the wealthier would just as soon keep them where they are. All this power play we owe, in one way or another, to Marx. It is "common sense"—common since him.

Again, the Bible says almost nothing about this type of struggle. It does defend the poor and question the motives of the rich. But it does not analyze the social situation in economic terms, and it offers no detailed economic solutions to the problems of the world. When the rich gouge the poor, the Bible calls it by the catch-all "sin," not "class struggle."

A pointed case is slavery. Slaves are found all through the Bible, and the New Testament sometimes hints there was conflict between the slaves and their owners. But the Bible does not resolve this conflict . . . except indirectly.

There is no doubt in my mind that the Bible did bring an end to slavery, though it took 1900 years to do it. The process was slow, too slow. But it succeeded. In the entire history of the world the first significant country ever to ban slavery was Great Britain. It spread the cause to other (reluctant) nations like the U.S. If you study both the arguments that were used against slavery and the lives of the people who used those arguments, you hit the Bible again and again.

The Bible says nothing of this class struggle, but it does give an answer. It says that all people are equal in God's eyes. It tells us to love our neighbors and not use them for our own purposes. Under the pressure of hundreds of years of that teaching, slavery crumbled. The Bible had a far better answer to slavery than Marxism did: as Solzhenitsyn bravely points out, slavery of a cruel kind has not vanished in Communist countries. Nor has it vanished in so-called Christian countries. But I think it is fair to say that wherever Christ is really obeyed, you will find people trying to break down the class distinctions that divide them.

I have referred to Freud and Marx at quite a length because I wanted to show something about self-image problems. Because the Bible says so little about the "why" behind the problems of men, a new theory can throw much light on the problems. Even if we don't agree with much of the theory, we can learn some things from it. This is true of Freud and Marx; it is also true of the new interest and insight into how a person feels about himself.

Problems of hating yourself are, it seems to me, as real as Freud's sex and Marx's money. Today we are offered new insights into those problems. The Bible needs to be applied to those insights: to rule out some, to refine others, to say "Amen!" to still others.

Though the Bible does not directly deal with self-image problems, once again it gives the right answers. And once again, the answers come in a familiar package: in the form of God's loving grace. For people who hate themselves, there is good news: God forgives free of charge. He accepts you as you are. He changes and heals you when you least deserve it. He loves you not because of what you are but because of what you can be. His love is free to anyone.

This eliminates certain cures to self-hatred. It eliminates the cure that simply tries to convince you of how wonderful you are. You *are* wonderful; but you are also horribly sinful.

It eliminates a cure that tries to make you a winner. According to the Bible, you can never be totally a winner in God's eyes without his help.

The Bible cures self-hatred one way only: through love, and particularly God's free love. Only this love, understood and accepted, can break the loveless cycle. "God loves me, so I can forgive myself." "God loves me, so I can begin to sincerely love others." ∎

Chapter 3:
WHAT IS LIFE FOR?

Advice For Eleanor

■ Suppose Eleanor, a college student, is so tall that every time she stands in front of the mirror she either laments or curses what she sees. In fact, she becomes so distraught that she starts to avoid contact with people. She becomes a recluse, a dismal, depressed, sour young woman. She loses all motivation for study and friendship and starts to fail in her school work. Then she is encouraged to talk her problem over with me. When I find out the problem, what should my goal be?

My goal is not to cultivate her self-love or positive self-image. To be sure, I would have nothing against her coming to like being tall. But that I regard as a superficial goal unworthy of a Christian counselor. My goal is to transform her values, namely to diminish the value she puts on height. I would try to convince her that her treasure is in the wrong place and that her heart is therefore starved, because it was created to relish something greater than outward appearance. I would not try to convince her that she is not really all that tall, or that people like tall girls, or even that she should like her tallness. Instead I would try to create in her a new hierarchy of values which would knock physical beauty out of its reigning position. The value I would seek to instill in its place is the surpassing value of knowing Christ, or better, of being loved by him. More specifically, I would try to get her to cherish above all things on earth the promise that for those who love him God works all things together for their good. I would seek to kindle a happy confidence in the ability and will of God to turn even her awkward height for her eternal benefit. ■

—John Piper
The Reformed Journal

Rising Hope

Rohn Engh

Searching For Happiness

■ Neal Steinhauer.
The gawky name to go with the skinny body
of a loudmouth
sitting in the football stands, hoping, please,
don't let me get picked last.
The jocks were choosing teams for P.E.
Someone heard his plea.

He wasn't picked last.
Next to last was more like it,
   and assigned to the track-and-field event nobody liked:
    the shot put.

Skinny Neal throwing a heavy steel ball?
He had no muscles for a muscle event,
  but he liked to put holes in the ground.
The heavy hunk of steel left his fingers,
  arched through the air
    and fell heavily,
      thumping a shallow moon
        into the wet Oregon grass.
He liked it.
Nobody told him to fill in the holes.
He could see his progress day by day, inch by inch.
Suddenly there was achievement ahead,
  a way to like himself and be liked.
For years he worked
  alone in the weight room
    alone on the practice field
      putting holes in the ground
        watching the distance grow
         watching the muscle grow
          obsessed with success,
            not caring what people thought.
All through high school he worked.
All through college too.
Then it paid off.
He burst on the national scene,
  became Super Duck, an Oregon somebody,
    a world-class athlete
      headed for Olympic gold,
        maybe an Olympic record, maybe, who knows,
        he would throw the shot to the moon.

He was pressing weights,
  straining under the massive load of lead,
    350 pounds.

A disc, a small, slippery piece of backbone,
    slipped under the strain
        in an agonizing *pop*.
He dropped the weights,
    fell to his knees, crawled out of the weight room
        in terrible pain.
Say good-bye to the Olympics.
Say good-bye to the records.
Say hello to being very average all over again.
He was bitter. The back got better,
    but not in time for the Olympics,
        and he never reached his best again.
His life grew angry.
He tore up weight rooms.
He didn't care about the shot put so much;
    he never could again,
        but what else was there?
He met another jock then:
    paralyzed from the neck down, permanently,
        the former world record holder in the pole vault,
            Brian Sternberg,
                hurt in a tragic accident years before,
                    now in a wheelchair,
                        permanently damaged,
                            yet permanently cheerful
                                and thankful to God.
Why?
Why?
Why? When he could achieve nothing,
    be nobody, go nowhere
        without a wheelchair?

Neal asked Brian why.
Brian said why,
    why because Jesus is worth more than all those things.
Neal took up Jesus with all the intensity
    he had the shot put.
And Jesus took him up, renewed his bitter, broken life.
Neal wrote,

DO YOU SOMETIMES FEEL LIKE A NOBODY?

"I don't regret those bitter years.
They taught me that it
   doesn't necessarily matter that you're reaching goals
      and accomplishing something.
Just any goal won't do.
Ultimately, it matters whether those goals are worth
   staking your life on.
Because I'd put my identity in something of very limited value,
   I ended up bitter and depressed,
      unable to handle defeat or injury.
Now I put my identity in the God
   whose value is above anything else.
He guarantees to support me
   whether I succeed or fail."   ■

The Dream Goal

■ What is it you want most out of life?

If you ask Americans that question, most of them will answer with a variation on one, almost obsessive theme: "I want to be happy." They don't want to be rich; they want "enough money to be comfortable." They don't have a driving urge to be president of something; they want "inner peace." It's as though the whole country, worn ragged chasing the American dream, now wants a vacation to "lay back" and "be mellow." And above all, to like themselves.

It's true for Christians just as it is for non-Christians. A standing feature of many weekend Christian retreats is the "self-image" seminar. It takes a bow to the Bible by pointing out that Jesus said we ought to love our neighbor as we love ourselves, so obviously we need to love ourselves. Where Jesus gave two commands—love your neighbor and love God—there are suddenly three, and this one takes priority over the other two. (This is dubious Bible interpretation, as we've seen.)

I see a contrast to this in Africa. Here, the question of whether or not you "like" yourself doesn't seem to have occurred to anyone. Most Africans are looking for opportunity, money, success, good lives, perhaps goals of "living up to expectations" which would seem fine to our grandparents but rather old-fashioned in America today. There aren't any "positive self-image" seminars crisscrossing Africa, as there are in America.

I personally think that the new American concern for inner

peace is primarily a good thing. But this is a good place to ask the question: Is being happy with yourself the greatest thing in life?

Suppose you became perfectly happy with yourself. Suppose you went to either a Christian or a non-Christian group that offered a self-confidence seminar and you learned to believe that you were good-looking, smart, and a natural leader. Then, because of your self-confidence, you became happier, made more friends, and did better in school. Would you have gained anything fundamentally important? Would your life now be OK?

Any Christian had better answer No. God is not likely to be impressed with your report card or the number of friends you have. Before God's judgment, no one will ask whether you're happy with yourself. It will only matter whether *God* is happy with you. And your opinion and God's aren't synonymous; what pleases you won't necessarily please him! Only success and happiness in loving and serving him will please him.

As a matter of fact, self-confidence can prove harmful. Many of the most self-confident people I know are far from having a good relationship with God. Some are so caught up in their own opinions and achievements, I don't think they would hear God if he used a PA system. God may need to break their confidence rather than build it up.

Neal Steinhauer needed to be broken. He had found a way to overcome his bad self-image. Through sports he became a somebody. He liked himself. But what was his life worth to God? Not much. I think I can say without fear that God is not concerned with shot put records. Only after Neal's self-confidence was completely broken was he willing to pay attention to what God considered important.

So what is a Christian's greatest goal? It isn't a feeling but a person, Jesus Christ. We want to know him and to be like him. He is not, if I read the Bible correctly, a smiling, peaceful guru. Buddha's image is more like that. You've seen his statue: round, sleek, eyes closed, with a self-pleased smile. That's quite different from the characteristic Christian image of Jesus on the cross.

What does the cross mean? It means nails in Jesus' hands

and feet as he suffers in the place of others. He is in agony, yet his eyes are open. He looks out over the crowd. He asks God to forgive his murderers. He talks to the thief next to him about heaven. He brings his mother and John together. He does not ignore his own needs—he asks God to accept his spirit, and in a terrible cry asks why God has forsaken him. But you can't envision him with the contented, self-preoccupied smile of Buddha.

Do you really want to be like Jesus?

If you want to be like him, you may first need to get past hangups of self-pity, a lack of self-confidence, feelings of ugliness or guilt. But then you need to go much further. At best, liking yourself is a Holiday Inn on the way to a far better place: to lose our own lives, as Jesus said, so that we can find them.

Think about Eleanor, the girl who was too tall. Her goal ought to be, as John Piper wrote, "the surpassing value of knowing Christ, or better, of being loved by him." Along the way to that goal, Eleanor will need to get rid of all the mental garbage she has stored up: self-loathing, fear, unwillingness to forgive herself for being "ugly," maybe the very awkwardness she has in the way she walks. But any improvement she makes in her self-image will only be in order to go on to a better set of goals, goals all Christians share:

To love God with all our mind, soul, and strength, and to love our neighbors as we love ourselves.

To enjoy all that God has made and called good, including our own bodies.

To accept and forgive people, including ourselves, on the same basis God accepts and forgives, still knowing all that is wrong and needing change.

To move closer and closer to what God wants us to be, and to trust that God has the power to take us all the way to perfection, living with him. ■

Chapter 4:

GOD'S FORGIVENESS AND OURS

Marty

■ When I was in the sixth grade, about to graduate to junior high, Mr. Melella gave our whole class a speech. He said we were all going to get a second chance. We would arrive in junior high with our records wiped clean. None of the old teachers' remarks which had accumulated in our files would go on to tip off our new teachers. "If you want, you can be totally new people next year," he said. "And that includes you, Marty."

Marty was always in trouble for smarting off or fighting. To teachers and parents he was the Kid Headed for Trouble. We kids knew that if there was trouble, Marty would get blamed. It occurred to me then that everything could instantaneously change. Nobody would know the old Marty!

But it wasn't long into the next fall before Marty had obviously failed again. He'd been sent to the principal's office, and it was to happen half a hundred times before we graduated from high school. The fresh start hadn't worked.

Somehow I doubt Marty got a truly fresh start. His "record" had been forgiven, but not the record that ran in his own brain. A truly fresh start would have to erase, not only the official record, but also all those built-up expectations of trouble that existed inside Marty. Without that, he didn't stand a chance.

But wouldn't it have been wonderful if Marty had really had a new beginning? ■

Making Up

by Jay Kesler with Tim Stafford

■ I was walking toward the pool, my towel over my shoulder, and met Elaine. "Hello," I said, and she fell on the ground and started crying.

I had no idea why. People don't normally respond to me like that. I sat down next to Elaine and asked what was wrong but she didn't answer. So I sucked on a blade of grass for a while, and eventually she turned to me.

"What's wrong?" I asked again.

"I'm the worst girl in the world," she said.

"What on earth makes you think that?" I asked, but she began to cry again. Feeling very awkward, I searched for something to tell her. "You know, there's a lot of competition out there. I could believe you're pretty bad, but the worst girl in the world . . . you'd really have to work at that."

"Don't make fun of me," she said. Then she told me about her last year.

"I was the first sophomore in our school ever to be a cheerleader. I got to go to all the upperclass events, and eventually I found myself dating a senior, the best basketball player in the school. We went everywhere together. Soon we were going steady.

"Then they had a senior ditch day, and I heard afterwards that he'd gone with another girl. We had a scene, right in the hall with everyone watching. I threw his ring at him and ran into the washroom and cried. I stayed home from school for two days, because I couldn't go and face my friends.

"One evening some girls drove by the house and blew the horn. They weren't the kind of girls I usually hang around with, but I was really low—feeling sorry for myself and tired of sitting around the house. So I went with them. We drove to a town about twenty miles away and pulled into a drive-in next to some guys. We talked to them and eventually paired off.

"The next day at school, there were stories about me all over the place. Kids at my school can be like cannibals. People want to tear you apart, and if you give them an opportunity, they will. The girls told people I'd done things I never had, and everyone believed them. No one would believe me. I said to myself, *If that's the kind of girl they think I am, then that's the kind of girl I'm going to be.* And for the rest of the year, I've been just that. I'm a mess. I'm the worst girl in the world."

As I listened to Elaine, I thought about what an omnipresent problem guilt is. Psychologists can talk themselves blue in the face explaining how unhealthy it is, but they can't escape the fact that guilt is real. Everyone feels it at times—maybe not so strongly as Elaine did, but powerfully enough. We've all done things we're ashamed of.

And when you're dealing with people who have deep feelings of self-hatred, guilt often turns out to be a part of the problem. You might convince someone that she is beautiful in God's sight even though she is tall. But how do you convince her that her sins make no difference to God? He hates sin, and she knows it. When talking to people who are tied up in self-pity or self-hatred, I've often found sin to be at or near the bottom of the problem.

It's a real thing: sin is real and guilt is real (though not all guilty feelings, by any means, represent real guilt). But how do you get rid of it so that you can have a truly fresh beginning?

Some people rationalize their guilt. They blame their actions on other people or on circumstances, and pretty soon they rub out the bad feelings their conscience gave them.

Your conscience is a very tameable animal. Adolf Eichmann, who destroyed six million Jews, showed almost no remorse. He said he would jump into his grave with glee, because he believed he hadn't done anything wrong. He'd tamed his conscience.

One favorite way of taming your conscience is what I call the "Harper Valley PTA" mentality. *Harper Valley PTA* was a song and a movie a few years ago about a lady who was being put down by PTA members. She went to their meeting and told them how bad they were. The implication was, "I'm better than you, because we're all bad, but I don't pretend to be better than what I am. At least I'm honest." Well, being honest doesn't count for much if you're just honest about being bad.

Most people don't handle guilt that way. They may excuse themselves, but when you get beneath the surface, they're like Elaine. They're really sorry for what they've done.

That's a necessary starting point. I'd rather see someone broken down with grief than arrogantly refusing to admit wrongdoing.

However, just being sorry doesn't necessarily help. It wasn't helping Elaine—in fact, it was destroying her.

Skid Row bums are sorry. It used to be quite a sport in Chicago to take visitors down to see them. You would roll up the windows, lock doors, and drive around looking at the bums lying in the doorways and gutters. You told your children, "Don't point at these men," so you drove along looking at them out of the corners of your eyes. You didn't want to embarrass them.

Actually, if you did what the bums wanted, you'd tell your children, "Point at them! Shame them!" Most of them were on Skid Row to punish themselves. They were sorry for something they'd done and were ruining their lives to prove how sorry they were.

Sadly, Skid Row sorrow doesn't help. In fact, it destroys you. Second Corinthians 7:8-11 tells us that. Paul's first letter really let the church at Corinth have it, and later he wrote something like, "I'm glad I made you sorry because it made you repent. Your sorrow was godly sorrow. But there is another kind of sorrow—worldly sorrow. And worldly sorrow leads to death."

The bums on Skid Row had worldly sorrow. So did Elaine. It was remorse—taking on yourself the responsibility for something you've done wrong and living with it. Nothing will destroy people faster.

You want to see clear examples of worldly and godly sorrow? Look in the Bible. Two of Jesus' disciples are perfect examples: Judas and Peter.

Judas is unquestionably the world's most unpopular man. What father ever looked at his newborn son and said, "I think I'll name him Judas"?

But this attitude sometimes makes us paint Judas in the wrong way. We think of him as a sneaky, traitorous, dirty little so-and-so who never had any intention of following Jesus in the first place. That's far from what Judas was like.

For one thing, he was the treasurer of the apostolic group.

You don't take the sneakiest person in the group and make him treasurer. You couldn't tell the disciples from other people on the street by the halos around their heads. You could tell them, however, by the absence of a bulge where a guy normally carried his billfold. Why? Because all the disciples gave their billfolds to Judas. He was chosen to handle the money for the whole group. They trusted him!

And Judas did choose to follow Jesus. I think he was sincere in wanting to help Jesus set up a new kingdom. He just lost faith and eventually sold out.

Many other people have lost faith in Jesus. Peter did, too, even though he was one of the disciples' "inner three." He was one of the few men in history to hear the audible voice of God, when God said, "This is my beloved Son; hear him." But that didn't keep Peter from making mistakes. He missed the point of Jesus' life so badly once that Jesus said to him, "Get behind me, Satan."

At the time of Jesus' crucifixion, tremendous pressure was put on both these men. Judas had been steadily losing faith in Jesus, and he did the worst thing possible—he betrayed Jesus for thirty pieces of silver. He felt guilty about it, and after they'd arrested Jesus, he tried to undo it by giving the money back. The Pharisees wouldn't take it. They laughed at him. With their laughter ringing in his ears, he threw the money down and ran out of the room. He felt absolutely awful. He thought of James and John and the big fisherman Peter. He'd spent three years with them, and now, how could he ever face them again? How could he ever prove to them how sorry he was?

At about the same time Judas was thinking this, Peter was going through a similar crisis. He'd told Jesus he'd never desert him, and when Jesus was arrested, he had followed behind him even though everyone else had run. Maybe he hoped to rescue him. He waited outside while Jesus was on trial and warmed his hands at the fire.

But when a girl came by and asked him if he was one of

Jesus' followers, Peter got scared, and he swore that he wasn't. It happened twice more that night—he did what he'd sworn never to do: he denied knowing anything about Jesus at all. And then he heard the rooster crow, and he remembered that Jesus had predicted he'd deny him, just that way. Peter fell apart. Peter, the big, strong fisherman, ran away weeping bitterly.

Judas and Peter had both blown it—and they both were sorry. But how did they respond to their guilt? Judas was determined to demonstrate how sorry he was. Eventually he thought of a plan that would prove it. No one would ever be able to deny he was sorry for betraying Jesus. He went as far as any man can go to prove he's sorry: he went out and killed himself. Scripture leaves no doubt that Judas is separated from God today. He was sorry, but his sorrow wasn't godly sorrow.

Peter's was. Was he more sincere than Judas? I doubt it. But the next time we see him, he's preaching at Pentecost, bringing thousands of people to faith in Jesus. What's the difference?

The difference is in the object of the sorrow. The remorseful man puts all the blame on himself and keeps it there. He turns inward, dwelling on his faults and sins. He wants them to weigh him down so he and everyone else will know he's sorry. That's what Judas did.

The repentant man—the man who's sorry in God's way—puts the guilt and the pain on the cross by trusting Jesus' forgiveness. He leaves it there and goes on following Jesus, trusting him to convert his faults into strengths. That's what Peter did.

People in southern Indiana tell a story about a man riding down the road on a donkey, carrying a 200-pound sack of wheat on his shoulders. Another man asked him, "Why don't you take the weight off your own shoulders and put it on the donkey?" He replied, "You don't think I'm going to ask the donkey to carry all that weight, do you?"

I think many kids have the same problem. They hear Jesus say, "Come to me all you who are heavily burdened, and I'll give you rest," and they decide to go to him. But they still carry the burden of all the things they're sorry for. They're like people washing up to take a bath. You don't clean up before you take a bath; you take the bath for the purpose of getting clean. It's the same thing with guilt: you don't clean up your own guilty life through self-sacrifice, self-punishment, and self-destruction so that God can accept you. You go to God first and let him clean things up. Sorrow and self-pity really don't please God at all. In fact, they get in his way. What he wants is godly sorrow that repentantly brings things to him and lets him keep them.

That's the story I told Elaine. I told her about Peter and Judas, and when I got done I said, "Would you like to pray?" She said she would. She said, "God, I'm embarrassed about all these things. I've tried very hard to tell you I'm sorry. I've been doing these things because I felt so bad about myself.... I've been trying to hurt myself. I know that Jesus died on the cross for my sins. He was destroyed for my sins, and I can't get rid of my sins by destroying myself. So help me, God, to accept that and follow you."

It transformed her. Maybe you've read the story Franz Kafka wrote, *Metamorphosis*, about a man who woke up one morning having turned into a bug. Elaine's experience was the opposite. She thought she was a bug, and she turned into a butterfly right before my eyes. Suddenly she looked beautiful, and her whole outlook was different. She'd stopped holding onto that sorrow, and let it go. She was ready to follow Jesus.

From the day you became a Christian, God knew you were going to blow it. It didn't make him kick you out.

Repentance is a constant relationship with God. You don't have to hide sin in a moldy corner. You don't have to work up to a big emotional "I'm sorry" scene. You just have to learn to walk in a spirit of repentance, where you're more and more aware of how far short you are of what God wants, but also aware that God will forgive you and give you the power to overcome. That's what godly sorrow is about—instead of leading to death, as remorse does, it leads to life—forgiven, free, precious life. You don't need to hate yourself because of sin. God doesn't. ∎

Temperament

So you're a perfectionist?
You can't be happy so long as
   there's a single fault in you
      or your world?
Why won't you take God's perfect Son
   and taste that perfectness
      you'll never get another way?
God is a perfectionist, too;
   he already finished your work for you.

So you're depressed all the time,
   just naturally?
You're the introspective type,
   and you see all the evil inside yourself?
Won't you watch the cross while that evil
   is killed and punished,
      and stop punishing yourself?
God sees the evil too;
   won't you see the good he gave you?

Robert Maust

Chapter 5:
ON BEING LOVED

Something Free

■ When my father died, my uncle took on the job of looking after me. For example, after high school, I couldn't figure out how to pay for college. Unexpectedly, an envelope appeared in the mailbox with a check for $50 from my uncle. It came almost every month after that. My uncle never mentioned it, and when I tried to thank him, he seemed embarrassed and changed the subject. I got those checks every month, all the way through college.

My uncle was never verbally expressive about his love, but he showed it to me through that check each month. Funny, at the time the money was hard to take. I kept wanting to prove myself, to work for him and to show him I had earned the money somehow. I couldn't just accept it freely and be grateful.

Sometimes I have the same problem accepting God's love. Christians use a word called "grace," which simply means that God's love is freely given, with no strings attached, like that $50 check from my uncle.

It's hard for me to take that. I'm used to achieving because I work at something. I get good grades or make the tennis team only if I drive myself.

I think about all the "religious" things I do: going to church, studying the Bible, trying to avoid sin, hanging around other Christians. Why do I do those things? Usually, the answer I

Gregg Lewis

come up with is that I'm trying to prove myself to God. I figure the more fanatically religious I am, the more he'll be impressed.

Because of grace, though, all that frantic activity isn't necessary. Oh, I'm sure God wants me to go to church, hang around Christians, and study the Bible—but because I enjoy them and they're making me a better person, not because I need to impress him. Grace helps me to relax, to trust God, to realize he's already impressed enough to call me "a gift that he delights in" (Eph. 1:11 LB). ■

—Philip Yancey

Grace

■ He loves you.
He forgives you.
Can you hear it?
Will you hear it?
Or will you hang on
   to yourself?
To self-hatred
   self-pity
      self-doubt?

The Cure

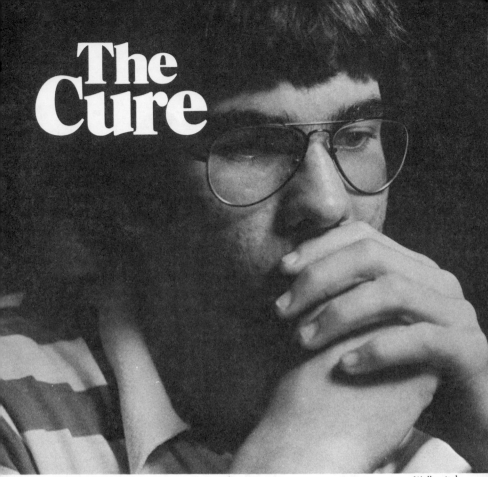

Wallowitch

■ I have scars tracing my cheeks in a coarse pebble grain, bumps and dents which mark where little red, pussy sores ran. Pimples leave scars.

But the scars on my face aren't the worst of it. They're so slight I can explore them with my fingertips and not feel them; I seldom think of them. The invisible scars on my mind, from shyness exaggerated by acne, are the most tender. Social illnesses leave scars inside.

I was painfully shy. I must have gotten it from my father who, although his job forced him to meet many people, never liked to. Always nervous at social affairs, he preferred to leave early if he couldn't get out of going altogether. (My mother, we said, would stay to talk to the pictures on the wall.)

Meeting strangers was pure terror to me. When I was twelve I had a job as a paperboy, and I liked the solitary early mornings on my bike, cutting corners just right, leaning backwards to blindly clutch a paper, and then heaving it on its way toward someone's porch, perhaps throwing a curve around a post, or angling the paper so it slid neatly ten feet to the doormat. What I hated was collecting money once a month. I would put it off as long as I could, then slink from door to door saying as little as possible, hoping as I approached each door that no one would be home. What should have been the best part of the work—the payoff— was by far the worst.

The day before school pictures were taken I might spend an hour in front of the mirror, finding just the right smile and then trying to memorize how it felt on my face. I never succeeded.

On top of the shyness came pimples, bursting on me at age fourteen like facial volcanoes. I was shy and doubtful enough about myself already: acne confirmed my suspicion that I was ugly. No one could tell me it "didn't look bad." I'd know they were lying. A dermatologist told me the only helpful thing. "It's not your fault, you know," he said. He pointed at my father, who had brought me. "Blame him. Your parents gave you those genes, and now you have to live with them." Still, I blamed myself. Those little surface sores bored straight through the skin to my soul.

But shyness was my worst problem. At lunch, clutching my tray, I would scan the cafeteria for familiar faces, always afraid of being left outside some protective cluster. It never occurred to me that everyone else felt the same way; it never occurred to me that I could strike out and become aggressively friendly. I only looked for protection and anonymity: the moment when a group parted slightly to accept me in and then closed around me without a ripple in the conversation.

I wouldn't be truthful if I left an impression of myself as a social misfit—one of those miserable few in every school who wander the halls, friendless. I was better off than most; I played sports, and I was a charter member of the elite crowd who ran the literary magazine and a few of the smaller clubs. I had a girl friend. I could carry on a conversation with even the most popular kids.

We always magnify our own problems, so now I see my shyness and acne as massive social blocks. Others probably weren't aware of them. We worry about what other people are thinking of us, when the truth is that other people are so busy worrying about themselves they barely even notice us.

And I have a good disguise for my weaknesses: cynicism. I am sure that I came across as sure of myself, impenetrable and arrogant. In some ways it was this disguise which scarred me most. Shyness makes us look vulnerable, hence very attractive; overcoming shyness can drive you to learn how to make other people comfortable. But covering it with cynicism, protecting it in a small band of shy, sarcastic friends, keep the self-hatred and the loneliness trapped inside. Wounds that should never have scarred deeper than the skin cut to the soul.

Now I can run a hand across my face and barely feel the acne scars. But when something in a conversation touches mental scars, I still wince. Do those scars have to stay tender? Do I always have to hide my weaknesses by pretending to be so sure of myself? I don't think so. Already the crustiness has softened, and I feel the scars fading. Just to write all this down would have been impossible a few years ago. The scab has fallen off the wound; the scars are fading imperceptibly to white, like old jeans. Something has happened.

Something has happened to set free those poisons trapped inside. Something is happening; I know that I won't be the same for long.

I explore my history through faded pictures of friendships and experiences. I can still pick out the faces; the memory of places and things come back sometimes with all the freshness of the original.

But I look in vain for a miracle. Something has happened to set me free, but what? No flash of insight revolutionized my mind; no friend in a single conversation healed me of all self-doubt; God did not startle me in the wilderness of my own bad feelings. Whatever has happened has come gradually.

So I'm tempted to prescribe what parents sometimes laughingly do: "Wait. Give it time. Your problems will go away." Will time cure a social illness?

I'm reminded of Ruth, whose problems didn't go away. Ruth is beautiful in every way: she's smart, people like her, and physicially she's perfect. You can look in her blue eyes and think how lovely it might be to be like her. But you'd better not look too deeply. Somewhere inside is a thick clot of self-loathing she can't cough up. Some social disease—I don't know what it was—left her mind paralyzed at the point of thinking herself worthless.

And I'm reminded of Johnny, who seems so hard and so smart. He's never given up that hardness; as a disguise for his fears, it's hardened into a permanent mask. Nothing has softened it; nothing now seems to penetrate it.

Time does not heal all wounds. Something has to happen.

So again I explore my past, trying to find what made the difference. Was it some self-help trick, a positive mental attitude, or a formula for making friends? No. All I find are a few strings running through all those years. They are strings which, if I tug, bring everything back to me, because they are tied to everything that's happened. And all the strings are made of one substance: love.

What happened was this: someone loved me.

It is such a simple thing that we take it for granted. In a list of things we ought to do, "love each other" often comes first but isn't thought about much.

I'm believing more and more that, in putting love before anything else, Jesus showed extraordinary wisdom. Love changes lives. You do not need a degree in psychology to use it. You do not have to thoroughly understand someone's problems in order to help him; love adapts itself to many circumstances and translates into any language.

Someone loved me. That has made all the difference and is still making all the difference.

Of course, you don't have to let love affect you. You can close yourself to it, from pride. You have to let yourself be loved. In all the changes that have come and are coming still, that is the only credit I can claim: I let it happen.

I let my family love me. In my case it wasn't hard, because there was good communication all along. Love and acceptance were always there. I know that's not true in many families.

Still, I know people who consistently pass up the opportunities that do exist. They pretend their family is irrelevant to who they are, cutting themselves off by always being too busy to try to hear the love between the lines.

But I doubt you can ever really understand yourself apart from your family. And I doubt there are many parents who really do not love their children. Many don't express the love well: they express it by nagging or threatening or buying things for you. But the love is there, and you have to let it touch you. Otherwise it can never heal you.

I let my friends love me. Perhaps the most significant thing I ever did was to find friends who loved. Sometimes people who feel sorry for themselves look for friends who will make up for them by being good-looking or popular or fun to be with. Tactically, it's a mistake, because those are the kids least in need of friends. But the biggest problem is simply that, as friends, they may not be worth much.

The friends who have mattered most to me have not been the most talented or the best-looking or the smartest. But they were willing to commit themselves to caring about other people.

Time after time I was able to break out of my shell because they took the initiative in caring for me and in being examples I could admire and imitate. I could probably have had friends in a more admired circle. But I could hardly have found a more caring circle. I let them care for me. I let down barriers that kept them at a distance. I let them know me.

I let God love me. Of course, he already did. But I had to let him into my life, not just once but many times. His love is not always easy to take. Sometimes it hurts to be loved, and it always hurts the pride. ("I don't need anything," we say and kill ourselves.) I let myself believe what he said: that my performance didn't matter to him, but only the openness of my heart. There were plenty of opportunities to discard him and let his love slip quietly out of my life.

I let myself love my self. That may sound strange, as though there are two "me's." But there seems to be two sides to each of us: with one side we want to love ourselves, recognizing the good God has planted in us, and yet the other side wants to drown that love with screams of dissatisfaction. We can focus on what we do right and can look for more opportunities to do it, or we can focus on what we do wrong and refuse to break out of the negative pattern we're in.

I let myself love me. I looked for good to happen. I became convinced that God was using time to make me better and that I could look into the future with positive expectations. I expected to see good blossoming in my life, so I took chances. I did reach out to people, overcoming my shyness. It was hard and painful, and it would have been nicer to sit home and nurse my sorrows, but instead I kept trying to enter the worlds other people lived in. The more I did, the easier it became. The easier it became, the easier loving myself became. I discovered that, at least for someone linked to God, loving yourself is the natural pattern; hating yourself is the twisted system that makes you work against yourself.

I have used the passive mood to describe what happened in order to make clear that I wasn't the doctor who invented the medicine. I only took my dose. However, I don't mean to imply that I sat at home, waiting for something. To get cured you have to go to the doctor and then to the drugstore, and you have to remember to take your medicine regularly. So I put myself in a position to experience love. I got close to those who loved me, and I let down my defenses to their love, and I began to love back actively, too. I had to be around the right people: close to God, to my family, to friends who really cared. That took action.

But the action only made room for the love which gave the cure. Love, which we take for granted in posters and greeting cards, which we use to sign our letters, which is the most common reaction to your first entrance in the world as a tiny, ugly, helpless creature—this ordinary thing is what we need to cure the crippling disease of self-hate. Love is around you: in your family, in your friends, in God, and in yourself. But you have to let it in. ■

Why Is It Good News?

■ What do doctors and police have in common?
They get to spread bad news.
Police ring the doorbell late at night. Someone comes
  in a bathrobe, sleepy-eyed, and they awake
    with the bad news: someone they loved is dead.
Doctors get to tell you you're dying of cancer.

No one likes to spread the bad news.

Everyone likes to tell good news.
You and your best friend both got an A on the test?
Guess who goes racing to tell him?

The first Christians called their message about Jesus the
   "good news" (translated: gospel).
The term was not thought up by a public-relations firm.
They were not trying to stick a pretty label on some nasty
   medicine.
They called it "good news" spontaneously.
Which explains, perhaps, why they spread it spontaneously,
all over the world.

We still call it good news,
   but we act, sometimes, like it's bad news.
We're reluctant to tell about it.
("I know I ought to.")
The meetings we have, where we talk about "good news,"
   can have all the joy of a morticians' convention.

The solution isn't, as some think,
   to slap on a grin and make everyone clap hands together.
You don't make it good news by pretending.
When you're honest with yourself, the question remains:
   what's so good about the good news?

Good news:
   someone you always wanted to know is in love with you.
That someone is God.
He loves you and will sacrifice anything to help you.
Being significant to God means more than being significant
   even to your best friend.
A friend can give you sympathy, but
   a God-friend can give you direction:
      he knows everything.
A God-friend can give you the power:
   there's nothing he can't change.
(And that includes the parts of you that are still
   bad news.)

"For God loved the world so much that he gave his only Son
   so that anyone who believes in him shall not perish
      but have eternal life."   —John 3:16 (LB)

"I pray that you will begin to understand how incredibly great
his power is to help those who believe him. It is
that same mighty power that raised Christ from the
dead."
—Ephesians 1:19,20 (LB)

Good news:
you're going somewhere.
Before this, all you were headed toward
was a tombstone.
Maybe you'd make a lot of money.
Maybe you'd do great things.
But in a few years, who knows? Who cares?
Good news: that big cold universe is Home
for God handcrafted it.
He has plans for you: he wants you to
participate in something that really matters:
something the earth was
created for, something that will last forever.
You're a key person in his eyes.

"Jesus said to the people, 'I am the Light of the world. So
if you follow me, you won't be stumbling through
the darkness, for living light will flood your path.'"
—John 8:12 (LB)

Good news:
Life is fair.
Some say the only thing that counts is whether you
make yourself happy with success, with money,
with admirers, with sex, with whatever it is you're after.
No one else matters.
You only answer to yourself.
That's bad news,
because it means the cheaters and the rapists
and muggers get exactly what they were after,
so long as they don't get caught.
And the mean-mouthed, the ugly-minded, the
utterly selfish, come out even better, because

there's no law against their crimes.
Meanwhile those who love, who sacrifice to feed
the hungry,
who care about people who are too abused to care about
themselves (old people, beaten children, mentally
disturbed, and those too low on hope
to ever pull themselves up)
get nothing.
And when you struggle to pray, to be kind, to love your
neighbor—you get nothing.
Virtue is its own reward—
the only reward.
But . . . there is good news about the future:
God is in control, and someday he will give rewards
for love, and rewards for selfishness too.

"It is to God alone that we have to answer for our actions."
—Romans 14:12

Good news:
you don't have to feel guilty.
If you could hear a tape recording of the thoughts
that went through your mind yesterday, would
they make you proud?
Mixed with a few noble thoughts would be
a long dribble of fears, sneers, envy.
You aren't what you could be. None of us is.
But good news is that you are forgiven the instant
you turn to God and sincerely ask him to turn
you away from your past.

"God has given us the privilege of urging everyone to come
into his favor and be reconciled to him.
For God was in Christ, restoring the world to himself,
no longer counting men's sins against them
but blotting them out. . . . For God took the
sinless Christ and poured into him our sins.
Then, in exchange, he poured God's goodness into us!"
—2 Corinthians 5:18-19,21 (LB)

WHY IS IT GOOD NEWS? 89

Good news:
   you can live forever.
You won't rot into fertilizer at death.
There is someone stronger than death,
   a man who converts an end into a beginning.
Jesus overcame death: he died. His body lay in a stone-cold
   tomb for three days.
He came back to life, not simply for a few more years,
   but eternally.
There is no more death in his life.
He offers his life to you.
Everyone is afraid of death.
We worry as though a huge clock were ticking in our ears:
   we don't like to think that everything we do can be
      cancelled by a broken valve in our heart.
Good news: death is a doorway, not a blind alley.
There is new life on the other side.
How do we know?
Because Jesus led the way.

"For all creation is waiting patiently and hopefully for that
   future day when God will resurrect his children. . . .
We . . . wait anxiously for that day when God will give us
   our full rights as his children, including the new bodies
      he has promised us—bodies that will never
         be sick again and will never die."
                                        —Romans 8:19,23 (LB)

Good news:
   there's a good reason to feel good about yourself.
When you think,
   really think hard,
      about all the good news God gives you,
         tailor-made to fit you,
            even utterly miserable you,
               just how long can you stay miserable?

If God cares so much for you,
   there's good reason
      to begin to care for yourself.   ■

Chapter 6:

MORE THAN FEELING

Holding
Back

■ It happened with shocking quickness. A student had given his secrets, his trust, his love to his girlfriend. Suddenly, she cut him off, with no other explanation than "I don't think it's working out. . . ."

He was deeply hurt. He was afraid, wondering if he could ever recapture the emotions he'd lost.

Sobered, he thought of different people he could trust with his secrets, his inner thoughts and dreams, without risking betrayal.

He considered his parents. But they'd misinterpreted him too many times. After tries at being honest with them, he had overheard them using a "yes, but listen to what our crazy kid thinks" example for the amusement of their friends.

He knew he couldn't trust his sisters, for they often turned on him selfishly.

He thought of others, more harmless—his feeble grandparents and the shy, ugly kid next door. But how could they return his love? What could he get back from them?

He thought of God—but could one trust even him? Didn't his own Son, in the moment of his greatest need, cry out, "My God, why have you forsaken me?"

He decided he could love no one without becoming frighteningly vulnerable. So he didn't. He lived in a shell. He went through polite roles of student, son, brother and friend, but never really exposed himself. It was as though he wore armor. He never reached out or responded to others' needs.

At least, though, he had himself.

He lived this way for years. One night after a deep sleep he awoke and found himself in hell.

It wasn't much different.

C.S. Lewis wrote, *"We shall draw nearer to God, not by trying to avoid the sufferings inherent in all loves, but by accepting them and offering them to him, throwing away all defensive armor."*

"To love is to be vulnerable." ■

—Philip Yancey

Bob Combs

Risking Your Life

■ You are in the cafeteria,
   balancing your tray and wondering
      where to sit,
         when you see someone sitting alone,
            anyone.

It could be a teacher
or the best football player in the school
or someone you've seen every day in Chemistry
but never met.
For a split second
with time pouring past
you stand wondering whether to sit
say hello
try the awkward beginning of a conversation.
You wonder whether you should take the risk,
the risk you might be rejected,
he might finish his lunch immediately
and get up leaving you alone,
the risk he might not talk at all,
the risk you might feel ridiculous.

We come to action now.
It's one thing to talk about
thoughts and emotions, quite another
to live them.
Thoughts come first;
this is the program Paul outlines in Romans 12:2:
"be transformed by the renewal of your minds."
As we listen carefully to God,
changing our thinking,
our lives also change.
Thoughts first; action after.
But if the thought never becomes action,
it's wasted:
You're like a ball in a pinball machine:
Up for a minute,
only to get banged around
and drop back to where you started.

You started with the self-pity cycle.
To break out you have to risk
reaching out to people.
In reaching out you forget yourself.
This is a practical way to apply what Jesus said:
die to yourself.

The result?
You begin to live.

Jesus told a story*
   of three men given money
     to invest.
Two gambled big
   and won big.
They doubled their boss's cash.
The third was timid.
Rather than risk,
   he hid the money
     and brought it through untouched.
Was the boss grateful for his caution?
Not a bit.
He said, "At least you could have
   put it in the bank to gather interest.
I didn't give you money to sit on it."
And he took what money he had
   and gave it to the others.
Jesus was saying,
   "You have to use what I have given you.
You have to risk."

But what if you risk and lose?
Jesus never told the story of the man
   who gambled his boss's money and
     lost it all.
That's right:
   There's no such character in the story,
     for there is no such character in Jesus' world.
In Jesus' world
   you cannot honestly risk
     and lose.
There is no person who takes
   God's talents and, using them,
     risking them, loses them.
No losers.
Only winners.

*Matthew 25:14-30

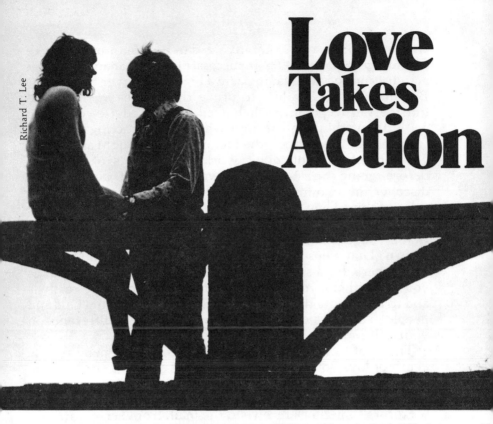

Love
Takes
Action

Richard T. Lee

I never knew anyone who changed his self-image simply by sitting and contemplating the beauties of God's love for him. People grow to accept themselves at about the same rate they climb outside themselves and actively care for others. If you struggle to like yourself, you must reach a point where you dare to leave your doubts behind and take risks with people. As W. H. Auden wrote to a sulking lover, "Act from thought should quickly follow. What is thinking for?"

This is why John wrote, "We love, because he first loved us. If someone says, 'I love God,' and hates his brother, he is a liar." When we grasp the sacrifice God made to love us in our ugliness, love begins to flow out of our lives. Love that comes in must go out.

A caution is needed here: action is not a short-cut. This is a mistake many counselors seem to make. They send people with self-doubts out to get involved in the community, make friends, get a partner. Their successful cases manage, through activity and social skills, to paste a big fig leaf over their fears. But many others, failing to prove themselves in the world outside, fall deeper into self-hatred. I would advise you not to act without thinking through what you are acting on.

In spite of this danger, the fact remains: thought and action grow together. You don't work up reserves of self-love before going out to involve yourself with people. You discover the two together as you go. They have a reciprocal relationship. They feed each other.

There are at least two reasons why they go together. One is that if you love other people, you tend to get loved yourself, in return. That helps you feel better about yourself and freer to love others. It's a spiral upward. The second reason is that as you love others, you begin to understand what love really is and to appreciate the love you have already had from God and people. That love can then sink in and make a difference in your self-image.

The depth of love you get will, of course, depend on the depth of love you give. If your love for others is shallow, the love you receive will be shallow too. You rarely get something better than you give.

Editors sometimes receive in the mail, from perfect strangers, butterfly stationery with notes written in green ink and signed "Love ya a bunch." I shouldn't pick on mushy girls, poor things, but they are an extreme that helps make a point. They do, indeed, "love ya a bunch." Cheery, anxious to help with homework or even knit you a sweater, who could be more loving? If loving actions automatically lead to loving yourself, mushy girls should never have a doubt.

But they do. When you get under the surface, they are often unhappy. They may have bevies of friends, but no one, they believe, really loves them.

I think people like that may be confusing admiration with love. The kind of love they offer others is the kind they dream of getting themselves, and it is very shallow. In their daydreams they are surrounded by adoring eyes. Their fantasies do not include piercing eyes that see their fluff and superficiality and pettiness, eyes that see truly and still care. They do not, for instance, often appreciate the love of their parents. They do not appreciate the love of God unless it is translated into a "neat" fellowship. They cannot bear any quietness in their relationship to God.

Nor have mushy girls mastered seriously loving others. They have a remarkable tendency to turn mean on a friend, to gossip, to get offended for life at an unintended slight.

There is a strong separation between admiration and love: they are virtually opposites. All of us, not just mushy girls, are tempted to prefer admiration and so lose out on love. When we dream of success, whom do we imagine—winning politicians? Movie stars? Successful authors? Famous surgeons? There are hardly four categories of people better known for selfishness, arrogance, and short-lived loves.

And when we think of people justly renowned for loving and being truly loved—mothers, for instance—do we really thrill to the glamour of being like them? Our preference for admiration over love is hardly surprising. After all, we crucified the truest lover of them all. On earth Jesus was loved by a few and admired by many, and, toward the end, loved by a few and hated by many.

It is common knowledge that you have to give in order to get. The greatest glory-hound in basketball knows that if he expects to shoot the ball, he has to learn to pass it. Masters and Johnson, concentrating on the athletic glories of sexual intercourse, learned that people who enjoyed sex most were those who tried the hardest to make their partner enjoy it.

I can't guarantee that if you love others they will love you back. Make it your business to love delinquents, criminals, dying people, or welfare clients and your returns may not be great. And certainly your love doesn't win additional love from God! He offers you the same love regardless of how you act. (So, in fact, may lovers, mothers, and devoted friends.) But I can assure you of this: if you really love, you will know what the tough business of loving is all about, and when love comes to you, you will recognize it for the incredible gift it is. Otherwise, you may be on the receiving end, but it will bounce off unnoticed. You prefer admiration.

I wish that I could find stronger words to stress this: if you are troubled by self-hatred, you need to learn lessons about love by putting it into practice.

That means, first of all, choosing people to love. God doesn't love by accident; you shouldn't either. You should think and pray seriously about people you know, trying to find one or two or three you can concentrate on loving. Of course, you don't have to stop trying to love everyone who crosses your path. But the serious, sacrificial love that God calls for won't allow you the time to offer it in depth to so many people. You have to choose people, or to be more accurate, find the people God has chosen for you.

Whom should you choose? God has made us each different. Some are suited for loving old people in nursing homes. Others would be better off staying away; they lack patience and the appreciation of age. There are plenty of choices, the lonely kids at school, jocks and cheerleaders, crippled children, even members of your own family.

After you've chosen, you need to formulate a purpose. I remember reading about a woman who had been moved by the plight of black Americans. She really wanted to do something to help. But after a year or so she realized her only plan of action was to put on a big smile and act very friendly every time she met a black person. If she was going to help, she needed to do more than smile.

Love is not a sticky emotion. It is an active force that changes lives. What should happen in the lives of the people you've chosen? How can you help them? Can you build their self-confidence? Broaden their outlook on life? Show them the meaning of deep friendship?

To do any of these things you have to be near them. It's obvious, but you won't be much help to people if you just drift along hoping to bump into them. You have to make plans to be in regular contact—and that may require asking the person you're loving to make plans, too. A few people can have a wonderful effect on people they only casually meet, but most of us must be there regularly, day after day.

When you are down on yourself, it's hard to get moving on an ambitious program. But at least you can start somewhere.

You can start with loving one person, in some small way. It could be someone already very close, a parent, a brother, or someone who sits near you in class.

The main thing is to move, to do something. You've heard about the astonishing love God has for you. That love demands a response. "We love God because he first loved us." If we will not respond to the love we hear about, we have in fact never accepted that love. We have rejected it. We have cut ourselves off from the only thing that can heal us, and gangrene is spreading through our lives. If our love never takes action, then we have no love in our lives. ■

The Only Lonely

■You say you're unwanted.
No one needs you.
Is that really so?
Are you the only lonely
   person in the world?

You say you've made it,
   feel okay about yourself.
You don't need to read
   about lonely ugly people.
Is that so?
Are there no more lonely
   people in the world
      who need you?

Jean-Claude Lejeune

I Wish I'd Reached Her

by Harold Myra

■ Lord, I never said anything nasty,
   but I admit I never accepted her—
      not as an equal.
She was a spinster at 17,
   and she always would be.
She reminded me of a skinny, leafless tree

trying to grow on an expressway divider—
    surrounded by concrete and grumbling cars,
        roots into grass so sparse and exhaust-choked,
        other life avoided her.
Even as a little kid,
    she must have been like that,
        alone, avoided,
            life roaring past her
                with no apology for the fumes.
Who hugged the girl but her mother?
Her face was angular, all bones, dark shadows,
    touches of black facial hair.
In a car full of kids,
    I ducked to the back seat
        to make sure no one got the idea
            she was with me.

She became very religious
    and even went off to Bible school.
I remember driving her somewhere
    while she was full of joy and resolutions.
"No Bible, no breakfast," she told me,
    saying how vital
        you were to her.
And that summer she got pregnant.
That was the end of her bright new life—
    you don't go off to Bible school
        with a baby in your tummy.
I wondered, then, unkindly,
    what hard-up misfit had touched her,
        had treated her like a person,
            had held her with affection,
                and suddenly nothing mattered to her
                    so much as being
                        held. . . .

I don't know about that summer.
But one thing she needed
    besides her Bible and prayers:

Christ to come alive in friends.
Could I have touched her on the shoulder,
    laughed with her?
Could the girls have been more like sisters
    than superior beings?
Maybe she could have found a love
    that wouldn't have left her pregnant and alone.
Maybe she could have been strong
    and chosen for herself,
        if she'd found more of you in some of us.

Beautiful kids have more fun, don't they?
They're the only ones who drink Pepsi,
    laughing like Nordic gods.
They're the only ones who splash down rapids
    with glistening teeth to commercial music.
They're the only ones who look so sexily tanned
    (are they the only ones with glands?).

You tell us, Lord,
"Don't be conformed to the world's standards;
    don't be pressed into its mold,"
        but it's been flashed into our brains
            in such volume the images drip over the edges.
And the grubby look of jeans
    can't change the mental machinery
        and the vicious social games we play.

Yesterday,
    I sat in a restaurant full of college kids
        and a group of girls noisily sat down.
They looked over at a pimple-faced guy
    two tables away,
        and I heard one snicker,
            "Oh, yuck!"
What a thing to say of a human!
How many times does a guy have to hear
    Oh, yuck!
        before he believes—really believes—

DO YOU SOMETIMES FEEL LIKE A NOBODY?

"I am garbage.
I am a walking, living, breathing
    pile of trash?"

A couple weeks ago, in this same restaurant,
    three guys and two girls came in.
One girl, fairly attractive
    slid into a booth
        and a guy slid in with her.
The other girl slipped in opposite them,
    but neither guy would slide in by her.
They looked at each other awkwardly.
Neither wanted to sit by her.
In a few seconds, one guy succumbed,
    but everybody knew it wasn't by choice;
        his reputation was safe.

I wonder, Lord,
    what those seconds did to that girl.
Did she feel like shrinking into her purse?
Did those snide hesitations
    move her toward hating herself?
Lord, why do you let a girl's beliefs
    about herself
        be found in her mirror?
One girl believes herself a princess
    and holds court.
Another girl believes,
    because of the shape of her nose,
        the toughness of her cheek,
            that she's a dog.
And it permeates everything in her life:
    this self-disrespect.
Lord, how could you
    put all those glands in her,
        those longings to be held,
            and have her clasp empty air all her life?

I WISH I'D REACHED HER

I read in a survey once
   that half the girls in America
      never land one date in high school.
Yet our culture screams,
   "A guy must touch you, kiss you,
      or you're not really alive."
You hear the cruel asides in locker rooms,
   "So many dogs around this school."

A girl rode our bus in high school.
She had orange, fuzzy hair,
   wore outlandish clothes from her mother,
      and she drenched herself in perfume.
I suppose she was saying,
   "Look at me! Look at me!
I'm not only human, I'm a woman!"
One day, she exploded at a senior guy—
   she couldn't articulate cleverly—
      it all came out in cliches like,
         "You, Mr. High and Mighty,
            you think you're everything!"
Later I asked her brother,
   "Have I ever given you that feeling—
      that I'm better than you?"
He never did answer me,
   but looked out the window at the trees.

I met this fuzzy-haired creature once,
   alone between classes,
      and asked her where a certain teacher was.
With just the two of us talking,
   suddenly we were two humans,
      like birds on the same rock,
         no audience to play to,
            no worries of who
               would be associated with whom.
She answered my question,
   and we talked a minute.
Although our words were no different,

DO YOU SOMETIMES FEEL LIKE A NOBODY?

the chemistry was altered.
For that moment. For about 90 seconds.
But never again.

How much have I grown, Lord,
   beyond seeing friendships
     as plus or minus status coupons?
Surely I don't still act that way!
But do I find more sophisticated ways
   to shun the misfit?

Do I love the nobody,
   the social embarrassment?

Lord, help me not to be molded
   by the world's ad campaign
     of luscious lovelies
       and wind-blown men on boats and horses.
By your Spirit, help me to see
   beneath the skin and posture, style and hair.
For I'm told you yourself, Jesus,
   were nothing for looks.*
But you sure are worth getting to know. . . .　■

*Isaiah 49

Plain, Scared Louise

by Ann Kiemel

■ Louise was the most scared, plain, little female student I had in my five years as dean of women. I always had a few, but I'd never seen anyone like this skinny, homely Louise. She came from a small town. She was very socially inadequate.

I believe she'd watch for me out of her dorm window, because I would drive on campus and three minutes later she'd be at my office door. She needed my attention, but it reached a point where it was unhealthy. I finally said, "You know, Louise, I'm your friend and I will always be your friend, but I'm not your whole life. Your life will be distorted and unhealthy if I let you become dependent on me and build your world around me."

I knew she'd cry, and I knew she'd be angry, but I knew that I had established enough of a relationship so she would know that I really loved her.

"Louise," I said, "in order for Jesus to ever really use you in the world, you've got to get out and plant little seeds. You've got to start learning to really relate to people, finding and doing what your thing is in the world."

Louise is a servant. She can bake, she can hem dresses, she can sew girls' formals. She would write in her journal every week, and I'd read it and make notes in the margins. Little by little, Louise began to blossom. I would love her but I'd keep pushing her out.

She would do all the little things on the dorm floor that

no one else would do. She'd clean out the little kitchen on the floor when everyone else left the dishes. She'd hem girls' dresses; she could alter anything they brought her. She would bake cookies; she would clean houses for people in the community of the college. In small ways she would love those people and they fell in love with her. She was the kind of girl that within her limits gave her best.

Now if you were just to look at her, you would have said, "She'll never get a teaching job." Never. No one would ever hire Louise. Period. Even after four years of college she was a nobody. No one noticed Louise. But when it came time for teaching contracts, she got a job. You know how hard it is to get a teaching position now, and the Boston area is one of the toughest. She looked as though she couldn't handle three kids, let alone a room of twenty or twenty-five. But she got the job, and her first year they asked her to be a supervisor over seven schools in several different reading programs.

She is fantastic. Third-graders think she's beautiful, and she knows how to run a classroom. Little, homely, ugly, unknown, insecure Louise. Suddenly she's blossoming and she's coming into her own. All because she was willing to give her best when there was no one to applaud.

Kids have grandiose dreams about doing great things in the world. But how many are willing to put their best into life *today*? Not so someday they'll get to be a movie director or a best-selling author, but because Jesus Christ is the Lord of their lives and they want to be full-hearted people. Without anyone to say, "I'll pat you on the head, I'll say you're wonderful, I'll give you a standing ovation, I'll give you an award."

Where are the people who are willing to say, "I will give today my best. Even if my best is sometimes lousy, all I can give is my best. Today I will give my best to life because someday I really believe it will make all the difference"? When you begin to add up thousands of ordinary days where kids have put their best into life, it does make a difference. ∎

—Ann Kiemel

BUSINESS REPLY MAIL

FIRST CLASS   PERMIT NO. 1596   WHEATON, IL

POSTAGE WILL BE PAID BY ADDRESSEE

CAMPUS LIFE
Subscription Service
465 Gundersen Dr.
Carol Stream, IL 60188

BUSINESS REPLY MAIL

FIRST CLASS   PERMIT NO. 1596   WHEATON, IL

POSTAGE WILL BE PAID BY ADDRESSEE

CAMPUS LIFE
Subscription Service
465 Gundersen Dr.
Carol Stream, IL 60188

Chapter 7:
WHEN THINGS STAY UGLY

Grandpa's Long Journey

■ He died this winter, after the longest, most painful journey toward death I've ever watched. Most of his life he had been a strong-minded, vigorous missionary, traveling by camel to remote Indian villages, preaching to stone-faced Muslims. I knew him later as a grandfather who loved dogs, brisk walks in the snow, a good joke. He was as alive as anyone I could imagine, so alive that when he died I felt as though someone had cut down a huge tree in the front yard. Everything seemed small, bare and shabby, because he was no longer there.

About ten years ago he had a stroke and became aphasic. That means that when he talked, it came out gibberish, and when we talked, he heard it as gibberish. His brain was still sharp, but he was cut off in sight of the world. His mind was a dammed river, streaming with jokes he couldn't tell, love he couldn't express, ideas he couldn't communicate. He had to live in a private, lonely world.

My mother managed all his finances, something that, as a Scotsman, he'd always done with rigorous pride. He grew weak, so in the end she managed everything: his dressing, his eating, even his urinating. It was hard for her, humiliating for him. He prayed to die. He longed for heaven. Yet he lived on, ten long years, ten years with hardly a word spoken or understood.

I often asked: What is the point of it? Why does God let him live on, torturing him so with a life that is useless to him?

Robert McQuilkin

Why not let him rest? Secret police sometimes torture a person by keeping him on his feet, not letting him sleep, for days. It seemed like that with my grandfather. Why?

I can only make sense of it by understanding that his life, even now, is not over. His work had not finished when he had that stroke; maybe it had barely begun. I believe in heaven, and I do not believe heaven is dull. (How could it be, with my grandfather there?) I think we must go there after life to work for God, at something so difficult, so joyful, so magnificently holy, that we aren't nearly ready to do it the way we are now. We need more faith, more patience, more strength. For that I believe my grandfather was being prepared. I believe he is working there now, talking eloquently while he works, smiling.

But that is my invisible hope. Visibly, there was nothing magnificent about the end of his life. He died with possessions that barely filled a small closet. He had no money or fame. He could do nothing. He had only two weapons left: faith and love. Stretched far into faith all his life, he was stretched farther by his condition. He never let his confused speech make him into a coward. If you greeted his beaming face in church on a Sunday morning his gentle, voluble conversation could startle you. He talked and laughed when most people would have been cowed into silence. And though no words were understood, much else was understood. . . much love.

Sometimes the frustration was too much for him. He grew tired and cranky. Christmas would come, and he would sit at a table filled with family who loved him, and he would be unable to communicate a single sentence, or tell a single joke. Sometimes he would cry. But then he would come back and be himself again, for another day.

Was he any use in those last ten years? To people, yes, a little. His broad face sometimes shone with such joy people found themselves cheered for having seen him. But mostly he was—and is—of use to God. He could not speak. He could not work. He could not even take care of himself. But he was still a man of God as great as any on the earth. ■

Clap~Hands
Happiness

■ I might as well admit it:
  some things change,
    some things don't.

David Strickler

Jill is a beautiful blond I know
    whose brain has been taken and tied in a square knot.
She's fine for a while but
    despite prayer and medicine and effort
        she falls apart
            about every six months.
Maybe her problems will someday fly away
    but more likely they won't.

Tommy is a guy I know
    so afraid he can hardly say "hello."
When he calls up and you answer the phone
    you hear silence.
"Hello? Hello?" and then you remember.
"Is this Tommy?"
A long wait and then he says, "Yeah. Hi, Tim."
Maybe his problems will go away (they've gotten better)
    but maybe they won't.

I know a guy with cerebral palsy.
He can't talk.
He can't walk.
His brain's all there, and he passed through college
    typing papers with his toes.
But I really doubt he'll ever be cured here on earth.
Some things change.
Some things don't.

Even for us with pimples, shyness, normal fears,
    a self-doubting personality,
        not good at school,
            not too good-looking,
                some things change,
                    some things don't.
You might always be shy,
    feel dumb,
        feel ugly.
You might struggle with it all your life,
    always fight to look in the mirror and like it.

You hear God's words of love and forgiveness,
  but still
    some things change,
      some things don't.

Survival.
Not a pretty word.
Not even a Bible word.
But it sums up pretty well words like
  patience
    longsuffering
      endurance
        which sprinkle the Bible.
Some of being a Christian has nothing to do with
  clap-hands happiness, the joy of the wonderful me,
    or Hallelujah, What a Savior.
Some is almost grim:
  hang in there
    don't give in
      keep on praying and seeking and
        knocking on doors.

That's not to say
  nothing can change.
I knew of a girl weeping and
  bemoaning her awful life
    (mean father,
      no friends)
        until her listening ear
          grew impatient and said,
            "How many of your problems
              are tied into the fact
                that you're forty pounds overweight?"
She was stunned, hurt, silent,
  until she admitted that ninety percent of them were,
    and she set out to change.
Not alone.
With friends to support her

she watched the pounds painfully
   vanish
      and with them her problems.
History is full of weaklings becoming kings,
   former flunkies elected president,
      uglies starring in movies.
Some things *do* change,
   and until you've wrestled to change them,
      with God's help and your friends',
         you've no right to give up.
But from the beginning know this, too
   some things change,
      some don't.

How come you always see old people in church?
They aren't much fun.
Aren't excited.
Just there, stuffing the pews
   gray hair
      gray suits
         gray faces.
They've got no future.
But maybe they teach something important:
   that church is not an amusement park,
      Disneyland of religious joy,
         but a spot where different people
            gather to wait
               and praise God together.
Wait for God.
The old people are closer to him,
   not meaning that they're more religious,
      but close because they will see him soon, when they die,
         and all the things they waited for
            will be theirs.
When we say "Wait,
   endure, hang in there,"
      we don't mean what others mean:
         "life is tough."
"Don't expect too much."

We mean wait for the celebration,
   your wedding reception with
      lions licking lambs clean
         trees dancing, waves clappng
            your family-friends singing and cheering
            and the lamb/lion Son of God
               Jesus
                  speaking "welcome" to you.
When we say "Wait" we mean,
   "Don't get confused with the wedding
      preparations;
         at the wedding it will all be happy.
Wait and see.
Someday you will see God."

There is another side to "Wait."
Paul wrote in Romans 5
   that perseverance builds character
      character builds hope
         which never disappoints.
Some things change,
   some things don't.
But while we wait God
   is working, making us
      his kind of people.
But how can I tell you? I don't suffer.
Listen, though, to the stories of people
   who struggle
      and survive
         and hope
            and give thanks.
If they can, why can't you?   ■

Bob

■ After the evening service at church, Bob Dye went to the Copper Kitchen to get something to eat, and he started crying. He couldn't stop. Big tears were rolling off his cheeks. "What is happening?" he kept asking himself.

He left the restaurant and went for a long drive around Medford, Oregon, going very slowly. Once he stopped and played with a stray cat who was investigating some garbage cans. "You're better off than I am," he told the cat. He kept wishing one of the passing cars would stop, or one of the dark houses light up and someone ask him in. He wished for the courage to throw a brick through a window, or to run his car up into the park and tear up the grass—anything for attention. Instead he drove over to the high school, into the parking lot and around and around a single post: slow, looping, pointless circles.

Then he drove home. It was very late, and his family was asleep. He went to his room, got some paper and began to write down everything he felt. The words tumbled onto the paper. He wrote several pages of scribbled feelings. But it all came down to one thing: God, I don't understand.

Finally, exhausted, he went to sleep. When he woke up he didn't feel much better.

Bob Dye has a "tic," or what you might describe as a series of nervous reactions. If he gets at all nervous, he can hardly talk. He makes a loud noise halfway between sniffing and clearing his throat, an explosive grunt. His head jerks, several times in succession, like a man violently flinging hair from his face. His shoulders jerk helplessly. It is a miniature fit which reminds you of the antics of a signaling third-base coach. Anyone might make any of the gestures, but when they come in rapid succession they don't look natural. In fact, they make most people feel very uncomfortable. And they are the source of the frustrations in Bob's life.

There is nothing physically wrong with Bob. He's been to enough doctors to know that, at least. He was born the son of a frustrated, unhappy man who wandered from job to job, sometimes working as a pastor of a church. His father began to hit Bob when he was three days old; when Bob was eight the family took a trip across the country and Bob remembers, movie-like, the image of a huge hand flashing time after time from the front seat, striking him on the face. Sometime during that trip the tics began to develop, perhaps as part of the impulsive jerking away from his father's hands.

He lost control of the reflex and began doing it unconsciously, especially when he was frightened of his father. And he was very frightened. He hated him. Memories that far back are scattered, isolated moments: he can remember going past his father toward his mother by slowly sliding around the walls of the room, as far from his father's hands as architecture would allow. When his father finally deserted the family, he left no money or support, but Bob kept some things his father had given: stored-up hatred and fear and grunts, tics and other nervous reactions he couldn't control.

There were problems in school, mostly due to the savage way kids laughed at him and mimicked his helpless actions. For two years he left Oregon and lived with his grandparents in California, because the school situation had become intolerable. When he returned to Medford in his sophomore year of high school, the teasing was no better. However, the longer he was there, the more others grew used to his behavior, so that finally they stopped making fun of him. But there were still barriers, and he always hated being in public near anyone who didn't know him: he hated the way heads turned to stare, especially when little children innocently stared or asked what was wrong. Anytime he went to a concert, he sat in the back, where no one would notice him.

After high school, he continued living at home. He went to college for a year, but ran out of money. One job has been followed by another—largely because of his tics and the consequent difficulties of getting along with people.

The best job was as an assistant in an auto body shop. Bob was supposed to buff out chips in the paint. However, the job was so exacting his nerves would start snapping and he would never feel confident it had been done right. He would keep working until a barely visible depression had been worked into the body, a depression that took major repair. His supervisor had no tolerance for his tics: sometimes he went into a rage and had to be held back from hitting him. Taking a finished car to a customer one day, Bob had a nervous twitch at the same instant another driver stopped in front of him. He plowed into the back of her car, and when he got back to the shop the boss said he would have to let him go.

Since then he's held several low-paying jobs. The state wanted to send him to a rehabilitation center, but after a two-day visit he found the place gave him the creeps. Bob has above-average intelligence, but no training for a skilled job. His nervous condition makes it hard for him to work effectively at precision jobs, or at jobs where he has to communicate often with other people. He is a consistently hopeful person, but his chances of finding work to match his abilities seem dim right now.

Bob's church believes strongly in physical healing, and Bob and members of the church have prayed for a change many, many times. Not only that, he has gone for help to pastors, youth ministers, parents, doctors, psychiatrists. He has spent hours talking to, among others, the Campus Life director in Medford. He has tried acupuncture and self-hypnosis. He has worked hard at learning to forgive his father, seeking him out after years of separation just to talk to him and offer forgiveness. But the problem persists, and it dominates his life.

There is some relief. Happy moments crop up in his conversation—a memory, say, of canoeing when he first arrived at college, three new friends (two female) in the canoe, and all the hot dogs and pop he could swallow waiting on the shore. There are moments when his prayers have resulted in a far greater patience and a sense of peace about his condition: he remembers those moments thankfully. He does his best to thank God consistently for life and its blessings. And he does say that without God he is sure that suicide or a complete mental breakdown would have befallen him. He credits God for life itself, for love, and most of all for salvation.

But he can't credit God for his healing, because it has not happened. His condition may have mental causes, yet it seems as permanent as a withered leg. It is no more Bob's fault than polio; who can hold an eight-year-old responsible for reacting wrongly to a violent, troubled father? The condition goes on: a persistent cage which imprisons Bob, taking up much of his thinking and dominating all his relationships. Bob still hopes for a miracle.

So why should you know about Bob? We all have troubles. But some have more troubles than others; for Bob, life seems like one sad lesson piled on another. It is worth knowing that though God may rescue some from that situation, others he leaves to struggle and suffer. But as Bob would be the first to tell you, God does not leave anyone alone, not even Bob. God's involvement in Bob's life has built a strength that perhaps couldn't be formed any other way. Bob knows how to endure. Perhaps it is endurance—waiting with faith, with continued hope in God—which counts more than all the friends we might have, all the money we might make and all the prizes we might win. Why else should Bob continue to suffer? ∎

Cindy

by Steve Lawhead

Pete Ceren

■ It's an effort to watch Cindy. Every movement is a study in determination, a struggle with nerves and muscles that won't obey. When she talks you have to listen carefully: the words are slurred and indistinct, often impossible to understand. Each word is a battle—for you and for her—and the words are strung together with great difficulty. Your mind races ahead to fill in the gaps or guess the meaning of the

DO YOU SOMETIMES FEEL LIKE A NOBODY?

sentence as it unravels. Communication is slow.

Cindy has cerebral palsy, a defect which dramatically affects the body and its movement, but not the mind. Cindy's mind is sharp, active, and aware. You wouldn't think that to look at her—most people don't.

She is trapped in a shrunken, spindly body that is out of control—literally. Something happens to the messages she sends to her legs and arms and hands; the messages get garbled, confused. Her brain tells her hand to move, to pick up a pencil—Cindy's hand jerks out and up, not in the right direction at all. Her fingers won't open to grasp the pencil; her brain has told them to close. Her hand smacks the table feebly. She tries again. And she'll keep on trying until she has that pencil in her hands.

Cindy's biggest handicap is not cerebral palsy—it's people who treat her like a vegetable. She has long ago come to terms with herself, the way she is. But others haven't. Usually, people only want to pity her, feel sorry for her. Or worse, they assume that since her body has trouble responding naturally, she must be mentally retarded. That, she finds, limits her more than the handicap itself.

She was older than most kids when she started school, fourteen by the time she reached the fifth grade. After the first week of school, the teacher called her mother and told her she was not to come to school any more. She was expelled. The teacher didn't want to take the time to communicate with Cindy. It was a bother having her in the classroom, so out she went.

Cindy was crushed. She had her heart set on finishing school with her friends. After a few months of talking to teachers and principals, and getting nowhere, Cindy got out some paper and wrote a letter to the school's superintendent. She wrote, "You allow kids to go to school who don't want to go. Why not one who wants an education?" The superintendent saw things her way and Cindy immediately entered the seventh grade, skipping a grade and a half. She regards that as a very big triumph, proof that she can function in an alien world.

But the demands stemming from her victory were almost

overwhelming. Homework. For most students, the only difficulty is deciding how long to put it off. For Cindy, just doing the homework often left her in a state of exhaustion. She had to type all her assignments letter by letter, word by word. It took hours every night just to type out a one-page assignment, an entire week to type an average term paper.

Somehow she kept up, progressing from year to year much the same as any other student.

She graduated from high school and decided to go to college, pushing herself to the limits of her endurance. It exhausts her to read and write for her classes, but she's making it. A recent operation, relatively new to medicine, is helping. In time she will learn to use muscles she has never used before. She will be able to walk and care for herself. That's a day she looks forward to.

But her basic outlook on life won't change. "God doesn't make mistakes," she says slowly. "Through him we have the ability to have an abundant life. I matter because I am his, and I have a purpose.

"I've always had a little trouble expressing my love for God. He is so tender that he gave an ugly little worm the ability to change itself into a beautiful butterfly, and so mighty he placed the planets in their orbits, and yet was so loving that he himself came down to earth and died for me.

"I look at the people around me who have given up on life—I look at Freddie Prinz. What a waste of human life! He had everything, but he wasn't happy; he didn't have anything to be happy about. Didn't he know he was important to God, that his life had meaning in God?" A look of puzzled disappointment comes into her eyes as she finishes speaking. She has more to say, but the words won't come now. She really doesn't understand why so many people give up so easily, accepting defeat when victory is waiting to be attained. And looking at Cindy, sitting in her wheelchair, remembering when she told me how she'd walked a mile and a half on her knees collecting specimens on the beach for a biology class, I think about that and I don't understand either. ■

Leo

by Philip Yancey

■ One thousand kids from all over California were gathered at a Campus Life Faith Festival. They had just heard a number of people expressing their feelings about themselves—ugliness, embarrassment, uncertainty. Then, without introduction, a film began to roll, flashing unsteadily on the huge screen before us. It was shaky at first, the sound track poor, difficult to follow.

Gradually the words steadied, "This morning begins the 24,373rd day of Leo Beuerman's imprisonment—not a prison of walls, but one of seclusion. . . ."

The camera focused on a typewriter Leo used, on watches he patiently repaired, on a Bible opened to his favorite book, Job.

The narrator spoke of a cart Leo made, and through the camera we moved outdoors, hearing of mobility and freedom. Sunflowers towered above us. A cow, curious, loomed menacingly close. Undetected by Leo's deafened ears, a train appeared, frighteningly close.

Experiences like these, said the narrator, convinced Leo's mother to keep him indoors.

We knew by now Leo was different, some kind of genetic freak. And then we saw him—a shriveled, twisted dwarf, all his features disproportionate, surely no more than two feet tall . . . the kind of person we're trained to look quickly away from.

Leo was shown on a tractor he and a nephew specially designed for his bent body. We learned that his mother had died by now, and Leo was alone, free to live as fully as his prison of flesh and bones would permit.

Every day meant a ritual for him. A painful and time-consuming ritual of manipulating chains and pulleys and carefully hoisting his tiny red cart onto the tractor. His hands moved awkwardly, never quite in the direction he intended. Screwing on a bolt was a tedious chore involving several tries.

But pain could be ignored. And Leo's time had to be filled somehow. So every day he made the pilgrimage on his tractor to town. There, once again, Leo carefully lowered himself and his cart down the complex ladder of chains and hoists.

After that, he was ready for business. Leo patiently waited in his cart, his wares—watches, pencils and pens—spread out before him. Adults, not wishing to stare at the handicapped, reflexively ignored him. His customers were mostly children and others who chose not to disregard the grotesque and deformed.

A proud "I guarantee it" sign, hand-lettered on Leo's cart, spoke his business philosophy. Leo never asked for charity, never took more than the advertised price for his wares. Independent and free, he had achieved his goal of being in business for himself, and he enjoyed life.

The film narrator spoke of Leo's determination: "An action need not alter the course of human events to be heroic." We saw Leo as . . . yes, "a unique creation of God." Leo didn't look on himself with pity and revulsion. Though imprisoned in his body, he found ways to transcend it. Actions we call normal—

like driving, speaking, typing, reading—to Leo were marvelous goals attained only by supreme effort.

But Leo attained. He drove his tractor 30,000 miles until his vision failed at age 66. Even blind and deaf in a rest home, he handmade leather purses to sell.

As a legacy to exceptional achievement, Leo left his thoughts, painstakingly typed:

"I think everyone at times feels lonesome, sorry for himself. But I'm not a quitter. Once weak and sickly, I'm now doing what no one thought possible. I'm in business for myself, enjoying life.

"Do I believe in the goodness of God? You all know the Bible saying, 'We know to them that love God all things work together for good.' So from my experiences in the past and to this very day, I can answer you truthfully, I most certainly do."

No one could have quoted that verse to Leo and comforted him in the midst of his adversity, because few have felt his kind of suffering. But the fact that Leo could still affirm God's goodness is a tribute to God's working in him.

Only thirteen minutes had passed when the film ended almost as it had begun: "And so ends the 24,373rd day of Leo Beuerman's imprisonment." Imprisoned, but freed to patiently exist, bringing glory to God.

The audience was totally silent as a narrator read from the Gospels, John 9: "And as He passed by, He saw a man blind from birth. And His disciples asked Him, saying, 'Rabbi, who sinned, this man or his parents, that he should be blind?' Jesus answered, 'It was neither that this man sinned, nor his parents; but it was in order that the works of God might be displayed in him'" (NASB). ■

All Creatures
Fat & Odd

by Bob Palmer as told to James Long

■ When I was thirteen I had a big problem. I was 5'6" and weighed 190 pounds. It doesn't do a whole lot for you when you're invited to the Rose Bowl to fill in for the Goodyear Blimp.

You can imagine what it was like going down the halls my freshman year in high school. The kids would see me coming, move way out, and say, "Look out! Here comes 'Fat Albert'!" always implying "Man, I'm gonna get crushed against the locker if I'm not careful."

Gym class was the most horrible and devastating experience of my life. I hated it! I was sick every day I had P.E. And to make it worse we had to wear those silly white gym suits. When I had it on I looked like the Pillsbury Doughboy.

My mother had to take the elastic out of my gym shorts and put in a drawstring so I could get on the largest size. I was the only kid in class with a bow in front.

And then there was the rope . . .

To this day whenever I see a rope hanging from a ceiling I'm wiped out. It was terrible. Most of those kids would go up that thing hand over hand like monkeys.

Then the coach would call out, "All right, Palmer. It's your turn."

"Clear the area!"

I'd start pulling on that thing, but I could never get off the ground. Finally the coach would say, "That's enough, the beam is bending."

I think I hated running even more than the rope, though. Our gym teacher was also the track coach. He had this thing about running.

Probably the most humiliating experience of my life happened one spring day during my freshman year. The juniors and seniors had their lunch during our gym class, so many of them were outside in the grandstands eating.

We were to run the 100-yard dash.

Now the juniors and seniors were never really impressed by the twinkie freshmen anyway, so they made all kinds of remarks to break up the boredom of their lunch.

But you could kind of sense the tension mounting in the air because my turn was coming up. They put their lunches down and looked toward the starting line.

When the coach called my name, I tried to bargain with him. "Now, coach, I've gotta talk to you for a few minutes. I got up this morning not feeling very well . . . ."

And I made all kinds of excuses.

He said, "Palmer, you're going to run."

"Okay, if that's what you wanna call it."

He put two other guys with me and told us, "When I say 'Go!' you go."

My running mates listened and did exactly what he said. The coach said, "Go!" And they took off.

But I was having trouble getting everything moving at once. I couldn't just go forward, I had to get my weight moving up and down first.

By the time I got to the finish line, the other two guys were already at the drinking fountain.

The coach came up to me, "Palmer, is that your *second* time?"

I said, "No, sir, it's my first time."

He looked at his stop watch, looked at me, and with everybody listening he said, "It took you nineteen seconds! I don't think anyone has ever run the 100-yard dash that slow. That's not a 'dash,' that's a tragedy."

The juniors and seniors in the grandstands were making remarks and laughing, so I just went around the end of the grandstands. No way was I going to walk by those kids.

I went the back way into the locker room before the other guys came in. I changed my clothes and then sat there crying.

I'm going to jump my story up several years later, when I learned the only effective way of handling physical handicaps.

I was working at a Christian camp. One Sunday afternoon this car pulled in, loaded with kids who had just ridden 400 miles. As the passengers piled out I thought, *Good grief! There's been an accident. But the car looks all right. It's just the driver who looks like he's been in a wreck.*

He got out of the car and staggered over to where I was. I had never been exposed to someone like this in my life and I didn't know how to react. He was an eighteen-year-old cerebral palsy victim. When he was born, the part of his brain that controls the small muscles of the body was damaged. As a result, he couldn't talk right, he couldn't walk right, he couldn't use his hands and arms right, and he wasn't good looking. I was amazed he could drive.

When he started talking to me, I could hardly understand him. He asked if he could stay at the camp all week. He hadn't pre-registered. He had just driven this carload of kids and wanted to stay with them.

I didn't know what to do with him, and we were full. "The only thing you can do is hang around till six o'clock and *maybe* there will be an opening," I told him. "But that's the chance you take."

At six o'clock I stopped at the office to ask if there were any cancellations. I was hoping there were none. But the girl said, "Yes, there's one."

He was so excited he got emotional over it because he was going to get to stay with his friends all week.

Well, his counselor came up to me after supper and said, "What in the world have you done to me?"

"What do you mean?"

"This guy you put in my cabin. I don't know how to handle people like him."

I told him, "I don't have any advice, so don't ask me."

The next morning the guys were all going to shave and shower to get ready for the day. Some of the guys were just standing there wishing they could shave when he came walking into the bathroom with an electric razor in one hand and the plug in his other hand.

Everyone stared as he jabbed out his twisted hand, then pulled his arm back and jabbed again trying to plug it in. He tried so hard. But he missed the socket.

The guys standing around didn't know what to do. Do we help him? Or do we leave?

Without saying a word, he drew back his hand, reached out to that plug, and missed again. About that time everything was getting very quiet.

Finally, he turned around and looked at them, looked at the plug, looked at the razor, and said, "Just call me Speed and Coordination."

The guys all laughed and thought, "Hey, that was good." But they still didn't know what to do.

He came to me about the middle of the week and said, "Bob, can I talk to the kids?"

I said, "Let me think about it."

The next day he was back again. "Did you think about it yet?"

"I'm thinking; I'm still thinking," I responded.

The next day he said, "Look, I don't have much time left here. I only have one day. Are you going to let me talk to the kids?"

"Come on out on the porch with me." We sat on the porch for a minute.

"Let's get right down to the facts, okay?"

"Sure."

"What are you going to do if I let you talk and you begin to drool and everybody's looking at you and they can hardly understand you? What are you going to do if some good-looking athletic guy all the girls have been hanging around like flies all week stands up and says, 'Man, I don't have to put up with this. I'm getting out of here'? What are you going to do if the guy leaves?"

He said, "Bob, that's not my problem. That's his problem."

That settled it. "Okay, you can talk to the kids."

That next morning he got up in front of the group right after breakfast. He tried to hold his hands still but he was nervous.

When he finally got his composure, his first words were: "I am what I am by the grace of God."

Everything suddenly became deathly silent. There wasn't a person in the room who wasn't hit by that statement.

Most of us hardly have our eyes open, have hardly learned to talk, before we start complaining about ourselves.

Something we don't have.

Or something that's not good enough.

If I could be in a different situation things would be better.

My hair's too curly. Or too straight.

My eyes don't go the same direction.

Here was a guy who never had a girl look at him once in his life and say, "That's the guy I want for my life."

. . . who never had the thrill of picking up a basketball and making a basket.

. . . who couldn't go into the pool and swim because he just couldn't get his body working right.

There he stood with that twisted body, saying, "I am what I am by the grace of God."

When he said that I thought, "Bob, you clod. You've never said that in your entire life. You've tried to prove to God so many times you could do it yourself. You've never really been thankful to God for who you are and what you are."

He continued, "You know, God doesn't just love the people who can eat right, because I can't. God doesn't just love the people who can walk right, because I can't. God loves me just as much as he loves you, and he made me just as unique as he made you."

I've seen a lot of physicially beautiful people who haven't given anything to God. Here was a guy with a wrecked-up body, but he'd given it to God.

Today he is head of a fantastic organization in Ohio. Five to six hundred physically handicapped and mentally retarded kids go to camp every summer because he gave his life to God. He built a residential home for the physicially handicapped. He has raised close to a million dollars all by himself to put all this together so that handicapped people could have the same experience of coming to know Christ that he had.

He stopped worrying about girls in his life. But God brought along a perfectly normal girl who wanted to love somebody for what he was, not for what he looked like.

After their marriage he wrote me and said, "Bob, for the first time in my life I'm a complete person. I have hands that can write and can feed me and do things that I couldn't do for myself. I'm a whole person, and God has done this for me."

I never remember that summer camp or that spring day in P.E. class without realizing how physical problems can so easily cause any of us to reject ourselves. Maybe we can't stand the physical home God put us in. We may say, "Hey, God, I didn't ask to be born. How come you stuck me in this? Why couldn't you make me more like other people? Why couldn't you make me someone everybody likes?"

The apostle Paul had an answer for that. He asks, "Who are you, O man, to talk back to God? Shall what is formed say to him who formed it, 'Why did you make me like this?' Does the potter have the right to make out of the same lump of clay some pottery for noble purposes and some for common use?" (Rom. 9:19-21).

Or as Phillips paraphrases it, "The potter, for instance, is always assumed to have complete control over the clay, making with one part of the lump a lovely vase, and with another a pipe for sewage."

Our attitude is, "Lord, I'll be a beautiful vase for you, but don't make me a sewer pipe. I don't want to be *that* common. I don't want to be one of those unnoticed people out there."

But sometimes God makes plain ordinary people like you and me. And then, too, he also makes the others. All kinds. Good-looking, funny-looking. Skinny ones, short ones. Even fat ones. And he can use us all. ∎